The Atlantic Ocean

THE ATLANTIC OCEAN

BY

CHARLES H. COTTER

GLASGOW
BROWN, SON & FERGUSON, LIMITED
52 DARNLEY STREET

First Edition - 1974

© 1974 Brown, Son & Ferguson Ltd. Glasgow, G41 2SG
Printed and Made in Great Britain

FOREWORD

THIS small work is designed to provide a broad study of all aspects of the fascinating geography and history of the Atlantic Ocean, essentially for the general reader.

The Atlantic is a major division of the vast, continuous world-ocean within which the continents of the globe are but mere islands. This great water-body, which supposedly takes its name from the mythical island of Atlantis mentioned by Plato, extends meridianally across the North Polar seas, from the narrow and shallow Bering Strait which separates Alaska from Soviet Asia, and thence southwards to the shores of Antarctica.

The north-south extent of the watery region of the Atlantic is no less than some 13,000 miles, which is about half the Earth's circumference. The area of the Atlantic, including that of its peripheral seas, is almost 40 million square miles, this representing about two-sevenths or nearly 30 per cent of that of the Earth's water-cover. It is the several aspects of this, the second largest of the three great oceanic divisions of the Earth, which shall concern us in the following pages.

Part I, which deals essentially with physical aspects, opens with a geographical description of the Atlantic Basin. This is followed by brief essays on Atlantic Geology, Atlantic Weather and Climate, Water Movements of the Atlantic, Atlantic Seas, and the Islands of the Atlantic.

Part II is concerned with human aspects, and opens with a chapter devoted to the Discovery of the Atlantic. This is followed by accounts of the Economic Resources of the Atlantic, and of Atlantic Trade and Commerce. The final chapter considers the Political and Strategic Background to the Atlantic Ocean.

CHARLES H. COTTER,
Cardiff, 1974.

CONTENTS

PART I

CHAPTER 1

THE PHYSICAL GEOGRAPHY OF THE ATLANTIC

1. Introduction

Scientists who make a systematic study of the oceans are at a disadvantage in that parts of their realm of study are not accessible to direct observation. Not being the natural home of mankind, the ocean is the least explored of the major surface characteristics of the Earth. Nonetheless, knowledge of the ocean has continued to grow and, at the present time, it is accumulating rapidly.

Although throughout the ages men have been interested in the sea and have sought to solve its mysteries, the modern scientific study of the oceans began as late as the 19th century. An important epoch in the history of the study of the oceans was marked by the famous voyage of the British research vessel *Challenger*, which initiated a series of voyages of scientific discovery at sea during the second half of the 19th century.

Challenger sailed from England in 1872; and, after an expedition lasting nearly four years, returned with a mass of scientific data concerning all physical, chemical and biological aspects of the ocean.

Following *Challenger*'s return to Britain in 1876 a commission was set up in Edinburgh with the assigned task of assessing the scientific results of the voyage. These results subsequently were published in 50 large volumes, which form a veritable library of oceanography.

The famous *Challenger* voyage opened the descriptive phase of the new science of oceanography, when the numerous data of the science were collected and classified. This era, and the important work achieved during its course, paved the way for the analytical study of oceanic phenomena which is proceeding at the present time.

Knowledge of the oceans has increased abundantly since the renowned expeditionary voyages of the 19th century. In recent decades, during which the ocean has become the centre of intense scientific activity, several national and international institutions have been established; and improved facilities—research vessels and highly-sophisticated instruments and techniques designed specifically for oceanographical investigations—have been made available.

1

Present interest in the ocean stems from a realisation that the sea and its bed are the repositories of considerable potential wealth in the form of food, industrial minerals and other resources.

The Atlantic Ocean, more so than the other oceanic divisions of the globe, has witnessed many important and exciting oceanographical discoveries in recent times. Our main purpose in this chapter is to present a broad geographical description of the Atlantic Ocean and its basin which will serve to set the scene for the other chapters of the book.

2. The Extent of the Atlantic

The Atlantic Ocean is one of the three oceanic gulfs which branch northwards from the Antarctic continent, the other two being the Pacific and Indian Oceans.

For most purposes of oceanographical study the continuous zone of sea which girdles Antarctica is considered to form a separate oceanic division, generally referred to as the Antarctic or Southern Ocean.

The northern boundary of the Southern Ocean is usually taken to coincide with an important geographical boundary zone known as the Antarctic Convergence, which lies at approximately 55° S.

The waters which occupy the Arctic Basin are also sometimes regarded as forming a distinct oceanic division known as the Arctic Ocean.

For our purpose we shall include relevant parts of the Antarctic and Arctic waters as forming parts of the Atlantic Ocean. On this basis the southern boundary of the Atlantic extends along the coast of Antarctica between the Grahamland Peninsula, which lies southwards across the Drake Passage from the southern extremity of the South American continent, and the meridian through Cape Aghulas, the southernmost cape of the African continent.

The eastern boundary of the Atlantic is chosen somewhat arbitrarily to separate the waters of the Atlantic from those of the Indian Ocean to the east. The waters of the Atlantic and Indian Oceans at this boundary are in free communication. The western boundary, which has a sinuous form, extends from Tierra del Fuego, eastwards through South Georgia, southwards through the South Sandwich Islands, then westwards through the South Shetlands and South Orkneys to Grahamland. In contrast to the eastern boundary, the western boundary has a geological significance (*see* page 11).

Stretching northwards from Antarctica through a distance, as we have already stated, equivalent to half the circumference of the

globe, the tapering Atlantic Ocean meets the waters of the Pacific on the other side of the North Pole at the shallow and narrow Bering Strait which separates the American from the Asian continent.

The islands of Greenland, Iceland and the Faeroes, strung across the North Atlantic between Europe and North America, form a barrier between the waters of the Arctic Basin to the north and those of the open Atlantic to the south. That part of the Atlantic to the south of these islands is roughly S-shaped. The Atlantic attains its greatest east-west width along the northern tropic between the coasts of Mexico and West Africa—a distance of some 4500 miles. The least distance between the African and South American continents is about 1500 miles between Cape San Rocque on the shoulder of Brazil and the coast of Sierra Leone.

Included in the waters of the Atlantic Ocean are those of its peripheral seas. In addition to the North Polar seas we include the Greenland and Norwegian Seas, Hudson and Baffin Bays and the Davis Strait, the Caribbean Sea and the Gulf of Mexico, the Baltic and the North Seas, and the Weddell Sea in the Southern Ocean.

Although the Mediterranean Sea is physically part of the Atlantic, it is so nearly land-locked as to constitute a physical feature on its own. The Mediterranean and the Atlantic normally are spoken of in contradistinction. For this reason we shall exclude detailed reference to the physical aspects of the Mediterranean.

The total surface area of Atlantic waters is about 40 million square miles. The estimated area of the Earth's oceans is about 140,000 million square miles, so that the waters of the Atlantic account for nearly 30 per cent of the total area of the Earth's water cover. This compares with about 55 per cent for the Pacific, the Earth's largest water-body, and about 15 per cent for the Indian Ocean.

The total volume of sea-water on the Earth has been estimated to be about 330 million cubic miles, and the average depth to be about 2000 fathoms or nearly two-and-a-half miles. Of the total volume of sea-water on the globe the Atlantic accounts for about a quarter, its volume being about 75 million cubic miles. It has been estimated that a cubic mile of sea-water contains in solution some 120 million tons of salt, and that the salt content of the entire world-ocean, if spread over the continents uniformly, would cover the land to a depth of about one mile.

The salt content of any division of the ocean is influenced by rainfall, evaporation, icemelt and freezing, and also by run-off in the form of rivers and streams from adjacent land-masses.

3. Atlantic Drainage

The Atlantic, although not the largest ocean, is the drainage receptacle for no less than half the drainage area of the entire globe.

It will be observed from a suitable atlas-map of the world that almost all the great rivers of North and South America—exceptions being the Yukon, Fraser, Columbia and Colorado of North America—flow into the Atlantic; and that all the rivers of Europe and most of the rivers of the Soviet Union, as well as the drainage of most of the African continent, feed the Atlantic. On this score the Atlantic, in terms of average salt content per unit volume, is the least saline and therefore, the least oceanic of the oceans.

4. Atlantic Coastlines

An interesting feature of the Atlantic, compared with the Pacific and Indian Oceans, is the high degree of indentation of its continental coastlines. Especially is this the case in the North Atlantic. Peripheral seas break up the European continent into numerous peninsulas, and long arms of the sea penetrate deeply into the continent. These, and the deeply-indented coastlines of Northern and Eastern Canada, and those of Central America—the latter almost enclosed by the long chain of islands stretching from Florida to the island of Trinidad off the coast of Venezuela—are striking features of the Atlantic.

The length of continental coastlines of an ocean, including that of its peripheral seas, compared with the area of the ocean is markedly greater for the Atlantic than it is for either of the two other oceanic gulfs.

5. Atlantic Bottom Topography.

The difficulty of sounding ocean depths was not overcome until the advent of the deep-sea sounding machine in about 1875. The essential feature of this machine is that thin wire is used for carrying a plummet to the sea-bed, compared with earlier sounding devices in which hempen-line was employed. The difficulty of sounding with a fibre sounding-line results from the friction between the line and the water through which it passes, so that at depths greater than a certain critical depth the force of friction exceeds the combined weight of the plummet and line. Depths greater than this critical depth cannot, therefore, be measured with a fibre-line. The piano-wire used in mechanical sounding machines is smooth and thin, but strong: keeping friction to a minimum, it enables the greatest of ocean depths to be measured.

Although ocean depths of several miles may be, and have been, measured by means of mechanical sounding machines, the task of doing so is extremely time-consuming and tedious. Many hours are necessary for each cast; and the problem of keeping the vessel, from which the sounding is being made, vertically over the plummet adds greatly to the difficulty of estimating depths using this mechanical method.

It is not surprising, therefore, that up to the year 1895 the number of soundings of depths greater than 2500 fathoms, which depth marks the dominant level in the ocean basins, was no more than about 500. The number of soundings of depths greater than 1000 fathoms up to the same time was about 7000. With such a relatively small number of soundings of oceanic depths, knowledge of the detailed topographical features of the deep bed of the ocean was impossible. It was not until after the invention of echo-sounding that bathymetric charts, as contoured charts of the seabed are called, became reliable.

A modern echo-sounder is capable of obtaining a continuous record of depths of the sea-bed over which the vessel on which the instrument is fitted has passed. The advent of this instrument marked a revolution in the method of charting the ocean floor.

For detailed study of the topography of the sea-bed at the present time, a device using echo-sounding principles, and commonly referred to as sonar, has been developed. This is capable of producing a three-dimensional picture of a relatively wide strip of the sea-floor. To a limited degree underwater photography is also used for examining the fine detail of the topography of the sea-floor.

We now know that although the detailed topography of the ocean floor is highly complex, the broad pattern of its relief is composed of three major surfaces. Each of these is separated from its neighbouring surface by a small, but marked, break of slope.

Some seven per cent of the ocean floor comprises the topographical surface known as the continental shelf. The continental shelf descends almost imperceptibly, having an average slope, on a global scale, of about seven minutes of arc, to a marked change of slope at an average depth of about 70 fathoms. This break of slope marks a significant geological boundary called the continental edge. Seawards of the continental edge is to be found the true ocean basins the waters of which flood the continental shelves. The continental shelf is regarded by some geologists as belonging to the continent rather than to the ocean-bed.

We have quoted the average dimensions of the continental shelf, and it is necessary not to lose sight of the fact that actual dimensions may depart considerably from average values. In the Atlantic, continental shelves tend to be narrower than their average width around Africa and along North and South America. In North-west Europe the continental edge, which lies relatively close to the coasts of Portugal and Spain, swings westwards in the Bay of Biscay and attains a great width off the British Isles. The British Isles lie, in fact, on the continental shelf of Europe which, in this vicinity, attains a width of some 500 miles. Off the Soviet Arctic coast the continental shelf has a record width of about 750 miles in the Barents Sea between North Cape and the islands of Novaya Zembla.

Relief features are by no means absent from the continental shelf: mounds, ridges, hollows and valleys are to be found.

Depths to seaward of the continental edge increase relatively rapidly along the second of the major topographical surfaces of the ocean bed. This surface, the average slope of which is a little more than 4°, is known as the continental slope, the total extent of which accounts for about 11 per cent of the ocean floor.

A puzzling topographical feature of the continental slope is the submarine canyon, many of which are to be found in the Atlantic. Many submarine canyons, which are long, deep gashes scored in the floor of the continental slope, are extensions of submarine valleys on the continental shelf. These, in turn, are often extensions of continental river valleys. We shall discuss Atlantic submarine canyons in Chapter 2.

The lower boundary of the continental slope, which is chosen arbitrarily, lies at a depth of about 2500 fathoms. The deeper part of the slope merges gradually into the third of the major facets of the ocean bed. This is the abyssal floor. Between about half and two-thirds of the total area of the Earth is occupied by the abyssal floor, which accounts for no less than 79 per cent of the total extent of the ocean floor.

6. Atlantic Ridges and Basins

During the preliminary surveys of the North Atlantic carried out a century ago, the remarkable feature now known as the Mid-Atlantic Ridge, was discovered.

The Mid-Atlantic Ridge is an S-shaped submarine mountain system extending almost unbroken for some 7000 miles roughly midway between the Atlantic shores. The greater part of the undulating summit line of the ridge has a depth of between about 1000 and 1500 fathoms. The ridge sometimes breaks the surface of the sea to form oceanic islands, all of which are volcanic. The ridge extends southwards from Iceland through the Azores, St. Paul's Rocks near the Equator, Ascension Island, Tristan da Cunha, to Bouvet Island near its southern extremity in latitude 55 °S. Oceanographic investigation suggests that the Mid-Atlantic Ridge is part of a global system of oceanic ridges.

The highest peak of the Mid-Atlantic Ridge is that of the island of Pico in the Azores. The height of Pico above sea-level is 7615 feet, but its height above the Atlantic floor is some four times this amount.

The Mid-Atlantic Ridge resembles any of the great continental mountain systems such as the Cordilleran and Andean systems of America or the Himalayan ranges of Asia. Investigation by lines of soundings reveals a complex ridge-and-valley topographical system with basins, plateaux and rifts, similar to continental mountain systems.

The only significant break in the Mid-Atlantic Ridge is a deep, narrow and steep-sided furrow, stretching for some 70 miles, having depths of as much as 4000 fathoms. This is the Romanche Trench, named after the French surveying vessel from which it was discovered in 1883.

The Romanche Trench is unique in that it is the only deep oceanic furrow which is not associated with a continental coast, as are the deep trenches of the Western Pacific in which the greatest of all oceanic depths are to be found.

From the outer boundaries of the Mid-Atlantic Ridge the sea-bed falls away relatively steeply to the abyssal floors of two great longitudinal oceanic troughs, the Eastern and Western Atlantic Troughs respectively. These flanking troughs are broken by lateral spurs which branch from the main ridge, and which form the physical boundaries of the several Atlantic Basins. Noteworthy among the lateral spurs is the Walvis Ridge which extends north-eastwards from the main ridge in the vicinity of Tristan da Cunha to the African continent a little to the north of the Tropic of Capricorn. The Walvis Ridge acts as a barrier to the deep-water circulation of the Atlantic. The Rio Grande Ridge, which trends north-westerly from the main ridge, also in the vicinity of Tristan da Cunha, meets the South American continent a little to the South of the southern tropic. This ridge, unlike the Walvis Ridge, is not continuous. A significant break in the Rio Grande Ridge allows the waters in the basins respectively to the north and south to be in free communication.

B

The main and lateral ridges of the Atlantic floor have a marked effect on the circulation of the deep water of the ocean: we shall discuss this in Chapter 4.

The northern extremity of the Mid-Atlantic Ridge merges into a broad transverse submarine plateau which connects the continents of Europe and North America. This is the Telegraph Plateau which separates the Atlantic basins from those of the Arctic to the north.

Connecting Scotland with the Faeroes, and extending westwards from the latter, is an important ridge named after its discoverer Sir Charles Wyville-Thomson. It was Wyville-Thomson who led the scientific voyage of the *Challenger*. The Wyville-Thomson Ridge has a maximum depth of not more than about 250 fathoms: it permits warm surface water to flow northwards, and prevents at the same time cold deep Arctic water from passing southwards, in its vicinity. The ridge has a marked influence on the marine life in the area and also on the climate of North-west Europe. Another significant ridge, having effects on circulation similar to those produced by the Wyville-Thomson Ridge, is the Iceland-Faeroes Ridge. To the north of the Iceland-Faeroes Ridge are the deep Norwegian and Greenland Basins which are separated from each other by an oceanic ridge on which stands the volcanic island of Jan Mayen.

To the west of Greenland, hemmed in by Ellesmere Island and Baffin Island to the north and west respectively and by the Baffin-Greenland Ridge in the Davis Strait to the south, is the Baffin Basin. The shallow sill in the Davis Strait has a maximum depth of not more than about 375 fathoms.

7. *The Arctic Region of the Atlantic*

A notable feature of the Arctic region is the expansive continental shelf on which stands the numerous islands of the Canadian Archipelago, as well as those of Spitsbergen, Novaya Zembla, Severnaya Zembla and Franz Josef Land.

The Barents Sea, Kara Sea, Laptev, East Siberian and Chukchi Seas, on which the Soviet shelf islands stand, together with the Beaufort Sea and the waters of the Canadian Archipelago, encircle two deep basins separated from each other by the Lomonosov Ridge which extends across the polar region along the meridian of 50° W. on the western side and the meridian of 140° E. on the other side. The basin on the Canadian side of the Lomonosov Ridge is called the Laurentian Basin, and that on the Asian side the Angar Basin.

The Angar Basin is connected to the Greenland Basin by a deep furrow which extends between Greenland and Spitsbergen.

In his epic voyage under the polar ice in the nuclear-powered submarine *Nautilus*, Commander Anderson of the United States Navy, sounded a depth of 2235 fathoms at the North Pole on August 3rd, 1958.

8. The Antarctic Region of the Atlantic

Diametrically opposed to the North Polar Basin is the continent of Antarctica. Dominating all other features of this vast continent, which is almost as large in area as North America, is the Antarctic Ice-Sheet. This immense glacier, having an average thickness of about one mile, extends across the south polar continent through a distance of about 2500 miles.

In the midst of the Antarctic winter, ice formed from the waters of the encircling ocean almost doubles the area of the ice continent. Freezing in winter-time and ice-melting in summer have a marked effect on the circulation of the waters of the three oceanic gulfs which stretch northwards from the focal zone of the world-ocean.

The Atlantic meets the Antarctic continent at a deep and wide indentation of the southern continent occupied by the Weddell Sea.

The waters which encircle Antarctica are driven eastwards by the prevailing westerly winds, and the current is strongest where the water is most restricted. This occurs in the relatively narrow Drake Passage between South America and the Grahamland Peninsula, where the width is a little more than 600 miles. The strong easterly set in the stormy Drake Passage was the principal difficulty to be overcome by ship captains rounding Cape Horn towards the west, during the age of sail.

Within a narrow zone to the north of Antarctica, in the vicinity of the 55th parallel, cold surface waters emanating from Antarctica meet southward-flowing waters from the north. Such a zone, at which surface streams meet, is called a convergence. At the Antarctic Convergence there is a marked change in the character of the surface waters and consequently in the marine life supported by the waters to the north and south.

The poverty of land-life in Antarctica is in striking contrast to the abundant marine life to be found in the waters which circulate around this ice continent. The cold, and therefore dense, surface waters in the extreme south flow relatively swiftly down the continental shelf and slope of the Antarctic continent, this process setting in motion a vertical circulation which gives rise to surface waters rich in oxygen, nitrogen and phosphate. The plentiful and constant supply of nutrients for the abundant single-celled plants which flourish in the cold waters of the Southern Ocean sets the scene for the maintenance of a complex pattern of biological activity in which the plentiful plant-life provides the sustenance for small species of fish, crustaceans and other forms of marine life. This, in turn, provides the staple food for larger fish, large numbers of birds, as well as marine mammals, such as the seal and whale.

9. The Atlantic Desert

Relative abundance of sea-life is closely geared to the vertical circulation of the ocean waters. In general, where sea-water rises to the surface marine life is abundant. In contrast, places where the movement of water is downwards tend to be the desert regions of the ocean.

One such desert region is the area in the North Atlantic known as the Sargasso Sea. This marks the central region of the major circulatory system of the North Atlantic, within which a gradual subsidence of surface water takes place. The Sargasso Sea, first reported by Christopher Columbus following his first voyage to the Indies, takes its name from the large masses of seaweed originally named Sargaço by the Portuguese. The seaweed, known generally as Gulfweed, is characterised by its grape-like flotation bladders. Gulfweed reproduces by a budding process: and, although its original habitat was probably in coastal waters it has, by evolutionary processes, adapted itself perfectly to its oceanic environment. Important life-forms in the Sargasso Sea are the multitudes of small marine animals, notably tiny crustaceans, which owe their survival to the floating rafts of Sargasso weed. For these creatures a lost foothold inevitably spells doom.

10. Trenches and Island Arcs

The abyssal floor of the ocean is scored in places by extremely long, narrow and steep-sided trenches in which depths well in excess of the average depth of the abyssal floor are found. The proportion of the total area of the ocean bed occupied by these deep furrows is not more than about two or three per cent.

The deep trenches of the ocean floor, most of which are to be found in the Pacific Basin, particularly on its western side are, in general, associated with festoons of oceanic islands which form island-arcs. The single island-arc of the North Atlantic is the Antillean Island-arc of the West Indies. This remarkable chain of islands stretches from Cuba through Haiti and Santo Domingo, Puerto Rico, the Leeward and Windward Islands to Trinidad, and thence westwards along and parallel to the coast of Venezuela. The only island-arc of the South Atlantic extends eastwards from Tierra del Fuego through the islands of South Georgia, South Sandwich, South Orkney and South Shetland, to the Grahamland Peninsula in Antarctica.

11. Bottom Deposits

The ocean bed is a region of deposition. Not only are the physical remains of marine life-forms deposited on the sea-floor, but the sea-floor is also the resting-place of much terrigenous material worn away from the land surfaces of the Earth, after this material has been transported to the sea through the agencies of river, glacier and wind.

Terrigenous deposits are confined almost solely to continental shelves and slopes. In general the coarsest material of this category of marine deposits is to be found near coasts, the particle size diminishing as distance from the coast increases. Beyond the continental slope, there are great quantities of finely-divided particles which form the marine muds.

On the abyssal floors of the ocean the principal marine deposits originate in the sea itself. These are the pelagic deposits composed of the remains of marine life-forms, largely microscopic organisms—both plant and animal—which flourish in the upper layers of the sea. These deposits, which are in the form of calcareous or siliceous skeletons, form as a result of what has graphically been described as the continuous rain within the ocean waters. The abyssal floor is one huge graveyard of the vast populations of marine organisms which inhabit the sea.

In the Atlantic the characteristic pelagic deposit is *globigerina ooze*. In addition there are significant areas of *diatom ooze* and *pteropod ooze*, as well as *red clay*.

The term *ooze* applies to a marine deposit composed of organic remains so finely divided that to the touch a moist sample feels perfectly smooth. The characteristic ooze of the Atlantic, covering about 70 per cent of the area of the abyssal floor of the Atlantic, excluding that of the Arctic Basin and the Atlantic parts of the Southern Ocean, is globigerina ooze.

The Genus Globigerina, of which there are numerous species, belongs to the Order Foraminifera of the Phylum Protozoa. The protozoans include the lowest forms of animals most of which are unicellular. The commoner forms of Foraminifera possess shells of calcium carbonate. Although most forms live at the sea-bed, a very important exception is the Globigerinae, which occupy the surface layers of the sea. They are very numerous in warm regions.

In general, globigerina ooze, which is cream, yellow or light brown in colour, is found at depths of less than about 2500 fathoms. Sea-water has the ability of dissolving calcium carbonate, this ability increasing with increasing water-pressure and with falling sea temperature. The tiny, delicate, discarded shells of Globigerinae dissolve completely, during their slow descent, before they reach the sea-bed at places where the depth is very great. This accounts for the limiting depth of about 2500 fathoms, where water pressure is very high and sea temperature very low, below which globigerina ooze is normally not to be found.

Diatom ooze is found in the South Atlantic in a region which is part of a belt which encircles the continent of Antarctica, between the parallels of latitude of 45° and 60° S. Diatoms are tiny plants, microscopic in size, which have the ability of secreting a siliceous cell-wall or frustule. Diatoms, of which there are thousands of species, have a preference for cold water, and prodigious numbers are to be found in Arctic and Antarctic waters.

Diatoms reproduce by a process of cell division. The cell content divides and the two halves of the cell-wall separate, whereupon covers are secreted on the unprotected protoplasm of both halves which then become independent organisms. The process of reproduction is very rapid and the number of new cells increases in geometrical progression. It has been estimated that a single diatom may give rise to about a thousand million independent diatoms within a month.

The siliceous remains of diatoms are almost indestructable. Although sea-water is capable of dissolving silica it does so very slowly, so that diatom ooze is found at depths exceeding those in which calcareous deposits are to be found.

Diatoms do occur in low latitudes at places where sea-water is cool at the surface on account of upwelling. A region of upwelled water, in which diatoms are to be found, occurs in the Atlantic along the South-west coast of Africa in the vicinity of Walvis Bay.

Pteropods are tiny animals of the Phylum Mollusca. They secrete calcareous shells usually spiral and conical in shape, and they flourish in large numbers near the surface of the open oceans, especially in warm water. Pteropods are sufficiently abundant in parts of the Atlantic to give rise to a characteristic deposit, principally to be found on submarine ridges (where depths are not too great), known as *pteropod ooze*.

At depths greater than about 5000 fathoms the predominant deposit is red clay. This accounts for about a quarter of the ocean deposits of the Atlantic, excluding the Arctic and Antarctic regions. Red clay is a finely-divided clay material, soft and greasy to the touch, and brown or red in colour. It has a low calcium carbonate content on account of the great ability of the very cold water at the very high pressure to be found at great depths to dissolve calcareous material. Red clay is composed of insoluble residue materials in the form of colloidal clays derived essentially from the land.

In regions of the ocean where icebergs melt, especially in parts of the North Atlantic where icebergs contain large quantities of material derived from the land, the solid morainic material rafted by the bergs is deposited on the sea-bed to form a characteristic deposit known as *marine glacial*. This comprises rock fragments of all sizes varying from large rounded boulders down to finely-divided rock-flour ground from the sides and bottoms of the valleys occupied by the glaciers from which the icebergs were calved.

Large areas of marine glacial are to be found in the vicinity of the Grand Banks of Newfoundland, this region being a meeting-place of warm Atlantic waters and cold northern waters which bear the Atlantic icebergs southwards into the shipping-lanes where the ice hazard in spring and early summer is the navigator's main concern.

In oceanic regions where strong prevailing winds are laden with sand derived from arid land surfaces, a characteristic deposit is that known as *marine aeolian*. A large area of the ocean bed in the eastern Atlantic in the vicinity of the Cape Verde Islands is blanketed with fine Saharan sand which has been carried thither by the north-east trade-wind known locally as the Harmattan.

CHAPTER 2

MARINE GEOLOGY RELATED TO THE ATLANTIC BASIN

1. Introduction

The most striking and puzzling feature of the Atlantic—obvious from a mere glance at a map of this ocean—is the almost perfect jig-saw fit of its eastern and western boundaries. This remarkable characteristic was noticed and remarked upon soon after the European discovery of the New World when the first crude maps of the Atlantic were drawn. The English philosopher Francis Bacon drew attention to the parallelism of the opposing coastlines of the Atlantic during the early part of the 17th century, and since that time this curious feature has been the subject of a considerable amount of scientific discussion.

Another puzzling feature of the Atlantic, also the subject of a great deal of scientific discussion, is the Mid-Atlantic Ridge, which we have described in Chapter One. This physiographical feature runs parallel to, and lies almost exactly midway between, the eastern and western Atlantic shores. The Mid-Atlantic Ridge extends from Iceland in the north to Bouvet Island in the South Atlantic, through a distance of no less than about 7000 miles. Some geologists consider the Mid-Atlantic Ridge to form part of a global system of oceanic ridges, and the present evidence certainly suggests that the Mid-Atlantic Ridge extends eastwards from Bouvet Island into the Indian Ocean, and northwards from Iceland into the Arctic Basin.

In this chapter we shall discuss some of the theories which have been advanced to account for the formation of the Atlantic Basin and for the physiographic features associated with it.

Within recent decades an enormous harvest of new material relating to geological history and to the present stage in the development of the Earth has been gathered. This harvest is sufficient in content and quality for geologists and geophysicists to establish working hypotheses relating to the Earth-sciences. We must not lose sight of the fact, however, that as time proceeds new evidence will come to light and this will support some of the hypotheses which have been suggested and disprove others.

It is not to be expected that the great puzzles of geology—

puzzles which have whetted the intellectual appetites of philosophers down the ages—are necessarily to be solved in this, our own, generation. The scientist seems to be ever on the verge of finding that ultimate truth which unceasingly he seeks; and the vanity of man leads him to believe that this is always within his immediate grasp. Although a tremendous store of scientific knowledge has so far been accumulated, there remain a great number of puzzles to be solved. It appears that there always will be urgent problems to challenge those who seek solutions. In relation to the Earth-sciences, what is sought is an all-embracing theory in which logical explanations of an infinity of observed facts find their rightful places.

The search for the reasons for the complex architecture of the Earth's major topographical features is an exceedingly difficult one. The scientific study of the problems associated with this search reach back no more than about 100 years; although at the present time these studies are advancing rapidly, numerous problems are yet to be solved.

Up to the time of the close of the 18th century it was widely assumed by scientists that the pattern of ocean basins and continents is a permanent feature of the Earth. With the progress of geology in the late 18th century and the opening decades of the 19th, this idea was to be questioned.

2. Hutton and Smith and the Beginnings of Scientific Geology

The two eminent geologists, James Hutton (1726–96), and William Smith (1796–1839), are credited with having established the foundations of the branch of geology now known as stratigraphy.

James Hutton recognised that sedimentary rocks are composed of weathered material from pre-existing land surfaces, and that most of this material is deposited in a sea-water environment to form marine sedimentary rocks. Marine sedimentary rocks include a wide variety of rock types amongst which are conglomerates, breccias, sandstones, mudstones and clays. Deposited with this weathered material, which is brought to the sea by the agents of erosion, are the discarded shells and skeletal remains of marine life-forms. The mixture of land-derived material and organic remains is subjected to pressure from overlying material and it is ultimately bonded together by cementing agents, these forming the matrix within which the fragments of deposited material are contained.

Subsequent to the formation of sedimentaries in off-shore zones, radial earth-movements result in sedimentary rock strata being uplifted so that they come to form continental rocks.

A sequence of marine sedimentary rock strata provides a fossiliferous record of past life on Earth during the period in which the rocks of the sequence were deposited. Because the succession of the rock strata is not generally unbroken, it being punctuated by periodic uplift and subsequent erosion of sedimentary rocks, the process of arranging the strata in chronological order is attended by considerable difficulty. The task of doing so, from a consideration of the fossil content of rocks which manifests the evolution of life-forms, is the principal preoccupation of the geological stratigrapher. The evolutionary process of life on Earth, which began some 500 million years ago, can be traced from fossiliferous rocks.

William Smith, often known as the father of modern geology, produced the first geological map of Britain. On a geological map the areal distribution of different rock strata is indicated. The inclination, or dip, of the strata to the horizontal at selected positions is indicated on a geological map. This information, together with knowledge of the relief of the area covered by the map, enables the user to visualise the solid structure and the vertical distribution of the crustal rocks of the area.

The foundation of Smith's work is based on two important geological principles. The first, which is known as the Law of Superposition, states simply that of any two sedimentary rock strata, that which was initially below is older than that which initially was resting upon it. The second principle states that each sedimentary rock stratum is characterised by its own particular suite of fossils. These two geological principles provide, for the stratigrapher, the means of building up the so-called geological column.

The period of geological history which has elapsed since the first fossiliferous rocks were deposited is divided into three major eras known respectively as the Palaeozoic, Mesozoic and Cainozoic Eras. The geological column is built up of a long series of rock strata which are grouped into geological systems based on age and fossil content.

The geological system in which the earliest fossils are to be found is called the Cambrian System. This is formed of strata which were laid down during the early part of the Palaeozoic Era. Rock strata of the Cambrian System were laid down during a long period of about 100 million years, commencing about 500 million years ago. Strata of the most recent origin are included in the Quaternary System which embraces the later part of the Cainozoic Era.

3. The Global Structure of Continents and Ocean Basins

Following the time when the foundations of modern geology

were laid by Hutton and Smith, and for much of the 19th century, most geologists considered the pattern of ocean basins and continents to be a changing one. This idea was suggested by the remarkable observed fact that marine sedimentary rocks are to be found, even in the central parts of the largest continental land-masses, thousands of miles from the nearest sea-shore.

The traditional theory of the Earth's history involves an Earth-body initially in a hot and fluid condition, which, since its genesis, has continually been in the process of cooling. These theoretical ideas were first advanced by Sir Isaac Newton. It was assumed that the Earth's body, at an early stage in its geological history, became rigid and that the subsequent contraction resulting from cooling, and the Earth's force of gravity asserting itself, created compressive forces, which, periodically, caused the upthrust of mountain ranges along weak zones in the Earth's crust. It was thought that the sialic continental blocks became fixed relative to each other at the close of the fluid stage of the Earth's geological history.

A curious feature of the distribution of the continents on the face of the globe is the remarkable antipodal arrangement of continental block and ocean basin. This arrangement led W. Lowthian Green to advance his Tetrahedron Theory, which was first published in *Vestiges of the Molten Globe* in 1875. According to Lowthian Green's theory the Earth's crust collapses, on account of the force of gravity, on to the more rapidly contracting interior. The shrinking continental crust, the shape of which has the least area for any given volume, tends to take up a tetrahedral form, the shape of which has the greatest surface area for any given volume. The corners of the supposed tetrahedral Earth rise above the level of the world-ocean to form Antarctica in the southern hemisphere and three shield areas of the northern hemisphere located respectively in Canada, North-east Asia, and North-west Europe. Between these shield areas, and occupying the faces of the supposed tetrahedral form of the Earth, are the principal oceanic basins.

On mechanical grounds a tetrahedral form for a rotating Earth is not tenable and the Tetrahedron Theory is, therefore, generally discredited.

In his *Das Antlitz der Erde*, which was published near the beginning of the 20th century, the famous Austrian geologist Edward Suess drew attention to the fact that there are extensive areas of the Earth's surface in which the oldest sedimentary rocks, of pre-Cambrian age, still lie horizontally disposed. These form the so-called Canadian or Laurentian Shield, the Baltic Shield, and the Indian and Angara Shields in the northern hemisphere; and the shields of Antarctica, South America, South Africa, and Australia in the southern hemisphere. Spread out between these areas Suess postulated the existence of broad zones of weakness in the Earth's crust. Folding and crumpling of the rocks within these zones, especially in marginal regions, are supposed to have been initiated by compressive forces in the crust arising from a contracting globe. Downward movement of parts of these weak zones, being more rapid on the contracting globe than the downward movement of the more stable shield areas, led, in some instances, to a transgression of the sea over areas which hitherto had been land. From a consideration of the ages of the rocks in the marginal regions of the shields of the southern hemisphere Suess envisaged these areas as being the remaining fragments of a vast proto-continent which included all the shield areas of the southern hemisphere and that of the Indian sub-continent. This proto-continent he called Gondwanaland, after a key geological province in India. The relative subsidence of what Suess regarded as weak zones of the Earth's crust he supposed to have given rise to the formation of the Atlantic and Indian Ocean basins during Mesozoic times.

Formidable objections to the so-called rigid Earth theory have been advanced from the fields of geophysics, and the idea of vertical motion alone accounting for the present pattern of ocean basins and continents is not any longer acceptable.

An hypothesis diametrically opposed to the contraction theory described above is one in which the Earth is regarded as being an expanding body.

The traditional idea of contraction was first challenged by the South African astronomer J. K. E. Halm, in 1935, in a presidential address to the Astronomical Society of South Africa. Following along the lines suggested by his studies of stellar evolution, Halm put forward the idea that the Earth's density is continually diminishing. During the youthful stage of the Earth's geological history, the material of which the Earth is composed was in a degenerate state, in that the atomic nuclei within the Earth were deficient in electrons. In this state the atoms are very tightly packed, this resulting in an abnormally high density of the Earth material. It was argued that atomically-degenerate material within the body of the Earth, in undergoing transformation to a condition of lower density, tends to cause the Earth to expand. Of course, the volumetrical effect of the transformation to a condition of lower density would be counteracted by the increase in the mean density of the Earth consequent upon cooling by radiation.

The hypothesis of a cooling Earth has, since the discovery of the process of radioactivity, been considered anew. The radioactive process applies to certain elements which are continually and automatically changing into forms having lower atomic weights. In the process heat is liberated. Radioactive material within the Earth gives rise to the production of considerable quantities of heat which, if not preventing entirely the cooling of the Earth by heat radiation, certainly reduces the rate of cooling through radiation. There is every reason for giving serious attention to the idea of an expanding Earth.

Geologists and geophysicists of the present time recognise the convergence of several lines of investigation which produce telling evidence of lateral or horizontal movement of the continental blocks of the Earth's crust relative to each other. This evidence has paved the way for the development of theories of continental drifting.

4. Continental Drift in Relation to the Atlantic Basin

In 1858, Antonio Snider, in his book *La Création et ses mystéres dévoilés*, explained the existence of plant fossils common to certain coal-bearing rock formations found in Western Europe and in Eastern North America, on the grounds that these continents were joined together during Carboniferous times when these particular rock formations were laid down.

This extravagant suggestion was not taken seriously. The idea that continental structures had drifted apart many thousands of miles seemed, at the time, too absurd to be considered, and the idea was to lie dormant for no less than half a century.

Some 50 years after the first appearance of Snider's book, the American geologist, F. B. Taylor published a theory of continental drift in 1908. From his study of the pattern of major faulted zones, especially those in the Arctic and North Atlantic regions, Taylor was led to suggest that two proto-continental areas were originally located in the North and South Polar regions respectively. Tidal forces were invoked, these supposedly coming into being as a result of the Moon's close approach to, and ultimate capture by, the Earth, to explain why the proto-continents fragmented and drifted apart. These tidal forces were regarded as providing the mechanism whereby the continental masses of sialic material were drawn equatorwards by moving through the quasi-liquid simatic material which forms the deeper layers of the Earth's crust. These forces caused, not only the fragmentation of the proto-continents and the subsequent drifting, but also the raising up of mountain ranges in regions of compression and the initiation of ocean basins in the regions of tension. The sialic continental blocks are likened to rafts drifting in a sea of underlying sima, this latter being in a plastic state to allow the solid and rigid rafts to pass through. Taylor elaborated his original ideas on drifting continents in a paper, published in 1928, entitled *Sliding Continents and Tidal and Rotational Forces.*

Little attention was given to Taylor's original ideas. In the first place geologists, although accepting the concept of lateral movement of parts of continental masses on a limited and relatively small scale, felt that it was unnecessarily extravagant to suggest lateral movements involving many thousands of miles. Secondly, the existence of mountain masses of more ancient date than the most recently formed mountain systems which, according to Taylor, resulted from tidal forces due to the capture of the Moon during relatively recent—in Cretaceous—times, leaves no way of explaining the cause of earlier orogenies—as mountain-building epochs are called.

Taylor's theory, like that of Snider's, although attractive in some respects, was based on insufficient evidence and suffered fatal objections.

Snider's attempt in correlating the fossil plants of Carboniferous rocks on the two sides of the Atlantic was part of a wider issue in the general sphere of historical zoology and botany. In studying the present distribution and evolution of life-forms it seemed perfectly clear to biologists that certain land-masses now separated by sea must, during past times, have been physically connected. Otherwise it would be impossible to explain the presence of certain species common to land-masses not now in physical contact. Some biologists postulated the existence of land bridges in certain positions at certain times during the geological history of the Earth. Such bridges, which could have provided migration routes for certain forms of land animals and plants, were invented to explain past and present distributions of animal and plant life. The alternative explanation of these distributions invokes the theory of continental drift.

Not only correlation of fossil plants and animals and that of rock types and structural patterns favour the general theory of continental drift, but other exciting fields of study provide converging lines of evidence which support the theory. The close study of past climates, or palaeoclimates as they are called, especially climates of places which in earlier geological times were heavily glaciated like present-day Antarctica and Greenland, has added weight to the theory of continental drift. Another field of inquiry, of relatively recent origin, is that in which the magnetic condition of sedimentary rocks is examined with the view to fixing the magnetic latitude of the place at the time the rock was laid down. The results of the study of rock magnetism, or palaeomagnetism as the science is called, provides compelling evidence of continental drifting.

Perhaps the name linked with continental drift most well known is that of Alfred Wegener, one-time Professor of Meteorology and Geophysics at the University of Graz. Wegener studied not only the geological history and structures of opposing Atlantic coastlines but also the palaeoclimates of the opposing shores. He produced a convincing catalogue of similarities which provided strong evidence that the Atlantic shores were once physically united. The results of Wegener's careful investigation were first published in 1915 in *Die Enstehung der Kontinente und Ozeane*, an English version of the original edition appearing in 1924.

To fit the geological and other evidence he had carefully assembled Wegener envisaged a single proto-continent, which he named Pangaea, which became fragmented some 200 million years ago during Mesozoic times.

The fact of the existence of the long mountain system extending along the entire western coastlands of North and South America suggested that the American fragment of Pangaea had drifted to the west: and the leading edge meeting the resistance of the floor of the Pacific Ocean, was subjected to compressive forces which gave rise to the formation of this major mountain system.

Assuming a westward drift of the American fragment of Pangaea Wegener felt justified in explaining that the West Indies island-arc, as well as the island-arc of the Southern Antilles, which extends from Tierra del Fuego to Grahamland, represent trailing fragments of sialic material in the wake of the drifting continents.

To explain the cause of the fragmentation of the proto-continent Pangaea, Wegener postulated tidal forces and forces arising from the Earth's spheroidal shape. He argued that the tidal forces on the upstanding continental blocks exceed those exerted on oceanic blocks of similar dimensions. The excessive tidal forces acting on the continental blocks cause them to move westwards through the simatic material which forms the floors of the ocean basins. This argument was aimed to explain the westward drift of continents.

The oblate spheroidal shape of the Earth was held to be responsible for the drift of continental blocks away from the pole, a movement graphically described by Wegener as *polflucht*. The excess mass of the Earth's equatorial bulge was held to exert a force on continental fragments which tended to drag them equatorwards.

The forces described by Wegener do in fact exist but their

magnitudes, as demonstrated by mathematical reasoning, are far too small to have the postulated effects.

The validity of most of the numerous trans-Atlantic similitudes which Wegener has catalogued, and the case for continental drift—despite the fierce controversy that persisted during the decade or so after the appearance of Wegener's book—gradually became respectable and acceptable to a growing number of scientists.

The eminent South African geologist Alexander du Toit has studied the concept of continental drift especially in relation to the southern continents. Du Toit, and other geologists working in the southern hemisphere, have sought to explain the evidence that a great glacier had, during the latter part of the Palaeozoic Era, spread over a large area of the now-scattered continental fragments which form the remnants of Suess's Gondwanaland. Using the hypothesis of continental drift, these continental fragments are regarded as having been physically united during late Palaeozoic times when Gondwanaland was heavily glaciated.

5. *Geophysics of the Atlantic Basin*

The new science of palaeomagnetism supplies evidence which favours the general theory of continental drift. The cause of the Earth's magnetism is not known with certainty. The first attempt at explaining terrestrial magnetism is said to have been made by William Gilbert, the eminent Elizabethan scientist, whose famous book *De Magnete* holds a prominent place in the history of science and technology. Gilbert demonstrated that the Earth acts like a huge magnet, and suggested that the Earth's magnetic field may be due to a large mass of permanently magnetised material within the body of the Earth. This idea is no longer tenable for it is now known that the temperature of the material below the Earth's crust is too high for it to retain magnetism. It is generally believed at the present time that the Earth's magnetic field is generated by electric currents in much the same way as a piece of unmagnetised material acquires a magnetic field when it is placed within a solenoid which carries an electric current.

The study of earthquake waves reveals that the Earth's core material has fluid properties. It is inferred that the Earth's core is composed largely of iron and nickel both of which elements have high electrical conductivity. Certain movements of the material within the Earth can generate electric currents with associated magnetic fields.

It is well known that both the direction and the strength of the Earth's magnetic field at any place on Earth vary with the passage of time.   Coupled with these variations the Earth's magnetic poles, at which the field direction is vertical to the Earth's surface, wander relative to the extremities of the Earth's axis of rotation.

The pattern of the Earth's magnetic field, as observed on the Earth's surface, is thought of as being due to the pattern of cells of convection currents of fluid material within the body of the Earth. Changes in the patterns of magnetic field strength and field direction on the Earth's surface are regarded as being the effects of changes in the patterns of convectional currents of core material.   In other words, the Earth's magnetic field, and the manner in which it is changing, provide clues as to what may be happening deep down in the Earth.

Support for the so-called dynamo theory of the Earth's magnetism has come from the researches of modern astronomy.   Astronomers have recognised magnetic fields associated with certain stars, in particular with that of the Sun.   From a study of the relatively dark markings on the Sun known as sunspots, the Sun is observed to be rotating with a period of about $24\frac{1}{2}$ days.   The highly-ionised material of which the Sun is composed is capable of conducting electric currents; and the sunspots, with associated phenomena called prominences, are certainly linked with convectional movements of solar material, as well as with strong magnetic fields to which these movements give rise.

Close and extended study of the Sun's surface reveals that sunspot activity undergoes a cyclic change, having a period of $11\frac{1}{4}$ years.   This is the period of the so-called sunspot cycle.   The general magnetic field of the Sun appears to undergo a complete cycle of changes in direction and strength during each sunspot cycle. The length of this period is doubtless related to the Sun's rotation speed and to the speed of the movement of solar material within the body of the Sun.   The relatively short period of about $11\frac{1}{4}$ years for the cycle of changes in the Sun's magnetic field is explained by the rapid rate of movement of solar material within the Sun.

Scientific observations of the Earth's magnetic field began in the early 16th century.   The interval of time that has elapsed since these first observations were made has been insufficient for scientists to gain a very accurate idea of the manner in which the Earth's magnetic field is changing over the long term.   It appears that the general magnetic field of the Earth undergoes a cyclic change in a way similar to that of the Sun's magnetic field.   The period of this change is very long in contrast to the relatively short period in the case of the Sun.   This is probably explained by the extremely slow

c

and sluggish movements associated with sub-crustal convection currents within the Earth.

The evidence provided by palaeomagnetism, which has only recently come to light, has enabled scientists to study the behaviour of the Earth's magnetic field for a long part of the Earth's geological history. It has been discovered that when certain sedimentary rocks are being laid down, and that when molten magmatic material solidifies to form igneous rock, the magnetic constituents of the rock align themselves in the direction of the Earth's field at the place and time of deposition or solidification. These rocks, therefore, contain and preserve a record of the magnetic fields prevailing at the times and places of their formation.

By examining the remaining magnetism of rock samples of the same geological age but from widely-separated continental areas, it has been found that the Earth's magnetic poles at the time of the formation of the samples appear to have occupied different positions on the globe relative to the present places of origin of the samples. The most satisfactory explanation of this apparent anomaly is that the places of the origin of the samples must have moved relative to each other since the time when they formed. The study of palaeomagnetism has, therefore, supported the concept of continental drift. Moreover, the results of this study agree with other geophysical studies, and this convergence of evidence has enabled scientists to reconstruct the geographical patterns of continental blocks for past geological ages.

Associated with the Earth's magnetic field are the vivid displays of aurorae to be seen in high latitudes especially in the North Atlantic.

Following the invention of a successful gravimeter for use at sea by the Dutch geophysicist Felix Vening-Meinesz in the late 1930s, gravimetric surveys of parts of the ocean bed have provided significant evidence which also favours the general concept of convectional currents within the Earth and continental drift.

In localities where the motion of sub-crustal material is vertically downwards deficiencies in gravity, or negative gravity anomalies as these are called, are to be expected. These localities are associated with the deep trenches which are to be found in certain parts of the abyssal floor of the ocean. The large negative gravity anomaly found in the narrow sinuous zone running parallel to the Antillean islands of the West Indies is associated with the Porto Rico Trench. A similar negative strip is associated with the South Sandwich Trench which is located in the South-west Atlantic.

In the vicinities of the oceanic ridges, the Mid-Atlantic being the best known, positive gravity anomalies are often found. This supports the idea that the oceanic ridges occupy regions at which sub-crustal currents move vertically upwards. Evidence which favours this view stems from the remarkable discovery that the flow of heat from the Earth's crust to oceanic waters is considerably greater along the line of an oceanic ridge than it is from the abyssal floor on either side of the ridge.

The evidence suggests that upper horizontal limbs of con-vection cells of sub-crustal material are, by frictional effects, responsible for dragging continental blocks laterally through the plastic sub-stratum. Along zones of divergence of convection currents, where sub-crustal material moves vertically upwards, sub-surface horizontally-moving convection currents give rise to rifting of crustal blocks and to the possibility of considerable local volcanic and seismic activity. In regions of convergence of convection currents, where material moves vertically downwards, the crustal rocks are dragged together and pulled downwards. It is thought that in such regions the deep oceanic trenches are located.

Associated with zones of divergence and convergence of con-vection currents are excessive geological rifting and faulting of rock strata and consequent seismological activity. All the evidence suggests that the Mid-Atlantic Ridge occupies a zone in which upward-moving convection currents diverge near the upper surface of the Earth's mantle. The ridge is a locus zone of considerable seismic and volcanic activity, and the geological and oceanographical evidence demonstrates that the ridge is a complex underwater mountain system scored with numerous rift valleys and lateral and transverse fault systems.

It has been argued by Professor Tuzo Wilson of the University of Toronto that, if the continental blocks on the two sides of the Atlantic have drifted apart on account of convection currents in the sub-crustal material of the Earth, the ocean floor on both sides of the Mid-Atlantic Ridge is built up of material brought upwards and which subsequently form the diverging currents which led to the rift of the proto-continent of which the present continents form part. Professor Wilson also suggested that volcanic islands origin-ally near the ridge might be dragged away from the ridge because of these sub-crustal flows. By comparing the ages of the oldest rocks found on Atlantic islands with the distances of the islands from the Mid-Atlantic Ridge it has been found that, in general, the Atlantic volcanic islands from which the oldest rocks are found are those which lie farthest from the ridge. Ascension, Tristan da Cunha, and

Bouvet Islands, all of which stand upon the ridge, are among the geologically younger islands of the Atlantic.

The curious system of lateral ridges which branch from the main ridge of the Atlantic is not easy to explain. Professor Tuzo Wilson has suggested that the Walvis and Rio Grande Ridges, both of which stem from the Mid-Atlantic Ridge in the vicinity of Tristan da Cunha, may represent chains of extinct volcanic craters, the oldest lying farthest from the main ridge.

The geological evidence suggests that the present system of convection currents within the Earth has maintained a fairly regular pattern since Mesozoic times. The rifting of the proto-continent, which appears to have given rise to the formation of the Atlantic Ocean Basin, is believed to have taken place during Cretaceous times about 120 million years ago. The rifting appears to have taken place about a fulcrum region located near the New Siberian Islands in the Arctic Basin in such a way that the continental blocks of the Americas and Europe and Africa have opened outwards like the blades of a pair of scissors.

The island-arcs of the West Indies and the Southern Antilles appear to be related to the Cordilleran Systems of North and South America. The Andean System of South America appears to be linked through the Southern Antillean Island-arc, to the mountain system which forms the backbone of the Grahamland Peninsula. The islands of the West Indies and the Southern Antilles have, therefore, a continental, and not an oceanic, origin, as do the islands of the Mid-Atlantic Ridge.

In recent times one of the principal frontiers of exploration has been that of the topography of the ocean bed. The traditional picture of the ocean bed was one of a monotonous surface with little or no relief. Knowledge gained by means of the echo-sounder—one of the most important of all oceanographical instruments—presents the ocean floor as a terrain having marked relief.

The topography of the ocean floor is no less varied than that of the continents. Huge mountain systems comparable with those found on the continents, isolated mountain peaks rising from extensive plains, long, deep furrows scored in the abyssal floor, and canyons as impressive as the great river canyons of the continents; all exist, although hidden from view, within the oceanic basins of the globe.

The sculptured features of continental surfaces have been carved by the geological agents of weathering and erosion. Wind, rivers and glaciers, the predominant agents of erosion of continental surfaces, are not available for carving the topographical features of the ocean floor. A great amount of discussion has arisen, therefore, in attempting to explain the forces which have been in operation to account for the varied relief of the ocean floor.

Of the various relief features of the ocean floor none has excited the imagination of oceanographers more than the curious submarine canyons, many of which are to be found deeply entrenched in continental slopes. Submarine canyons are very similar in character to the river canyons of the continents, and many are no less impressive than the famous Colorado Canyon of the United States of America. They are deep and steep-sided valleys often extending for many hundreds of miles, and which terminate on the abyssal floor of the ocean.

One of the many theories advanced in an attempt to explain the cause of submarine canyons suggests that they were carved by vigorous river erosion in times of glacial maxima when great quantities of water were locked up in continental ice-caps resulting in the sea-level being considerably lower than it is at the present time. The depths of parts of some submarine canyons are so great that it seems impossible for the sea-level to have been lowered sufficiently for river action to have been instrumental in carving them. It is true that many submarine canyons are accordant with present-day river valleys. The Hudson, which flows into New York Harbour, the Congo of West Africa, and the Loire of northern France, are examples of present-day river valleys which lead into impressive submarine canyons. On the other hand, many submarine canyons are in no way connected with continental river systems. The explanation of the presence of submarine canyons in the Mediterranean Basin cannot easily be explained by invoking a lowering of sea-level, on account of the relatively shallow sill at the Strait of Gibraltar.

During the last century it was suggested that a steep-sided canyon in the Swiss Lake Leman may have been excavated by a silt-laden stream running along the lake bottom. The suggestion received little attention until it was revived during the 1930s by the eminent American geologist Professor R. A. Daly. The Dutch geologist Professor P. H. Keunen has been prominent in devising illuminating laboratory experiments designed to demonstrate the effect of so-called turbidity currents on the ocean bed.

Core samplers, by means of which oceanographers are able to procure cores of oceanic sediments up to a thickness of no less than about 100 feet, have provided evidence of shallow-water deposits in regions of very deep water where shallow-water deposits are not expected to be found. This evidence raised the question as to how this material found its way to the place from which it has been recovered.

During the recent ice-age swift-flowing continental rivers, having had their base levels of erosion lowered considerably through oceanic waters being locked up in continental ice-caps must have carried immense quantities of land-waste in the form of mud, sand and gravel, to the adjacent ocean. It is now thought that much of this river-borne material flowed, by action of the force of gravity, down the continental slope in such a way that submarine canyons were excavated. Such submarine currents are the turbidity currents referred to above.

A turbidity current may be initiated by an earthquake, which may lead to movement of accumulated terrigenous material from the continental shelf where it has initially been deposited, to the adjacent continental slope on the surface of which a canyon may be excavated by the erosive power of the laden current.

The American oceanographers M. Ewing and B. C. Heezen, by investigating the records of breaks in Atlantic telegraph cables, have provided ample evidence that many cable breaks were due to turbidity currents, many of which were triggered off by earthquakes.

Professor Heezen has recently drawn attention to a mid-ocean submarine canyon which extends from the vicinity of Greenland southwards to the parallel of latitude of 38° North.

CHAPTER 3

ATLANTIC WEATHER AND CLIMATE

1. Introduction.

The state of the atmosphere at any given time, especially as it affects people in their day-to-day lives, is referred to as weather. The principal determinants of weather are air pressure, air temperature and air humidity, at sea-level and at higher levels in the atmosphere. These determine whether the weather is warm or cold, dry or wet, cloudy or cloudless, calm or windy, foggy or clear, and so on.

In general, the weather at any given place continually changes from week to week, from day to day, or even from hour to hour. The weather for any given time and given place may be expressed in terms of measured quantities including air temperature, pressure, humidity, wind-speed and direction, together with an indication of the state of the sky, and whether or not there is precipitation or fog. These measurements and indications constitute meteorological observations.

By synthesising and averaging meteorological observations made in any given locality from a sufficiently long record of such observations, that is to say, by eliminating the time element of weather, meteorologists arrive at a result called the climate of the locality.

Meteorlologists and climatologists study the inter-relationships of, and the interactions between, the so-called elements of weather and climate. These include air temperature, pressure and humidity. These scientists also consider how these elements are affected by the so-called factors of weather and climate. Over the oceans the principal factors of weather and climate are latitude, presence of ice, proximity to continents, and horizontal and vertical movements of oceanic water.

The atmosphere, which envelops the lithosphere and hydrosphere, is a mixture of gases which includes a variable amount of water-vapour. Water-vapour in the atmosphere, as well as the myriads of tiny particles of dust, salt and ice, which are borne aloft by the air, play important roles in respect of the state of the weather.

The atmosphere comprises a series of concentric shells. The lowermost shell, in which all terrestrial land animals are immersed, is characterised by an almost constant lapse rate, that is to say, by an almost uniform fall of air temperature with increasing height above sea-level. All the changes associated with weather take place solely within the lowermost atmospheric shell, for which reason this shell is called the troposphere, from the Greek word *tropien*, meaning 'to change'. The troposphere is the turbulent region of the atmosphere where clouds, gales, cloudbursts and lightning, occur.

The troposphere has a vertical thickness which varies with latitude, being about 11 miles at the Equator and about five miles at either pole. At its outer limit the air temperature is about −60° C. Above the troposphere the air is dry and the temperature is constant, at least for some considerable distance above the boundary surface or tropopause. Because weather is essentially a phenomenon of the troposphere we shall confine our attention solely to this atmospheric shell.

Almost all energy available on the Earth is derived from the Sun. Our nearest star emits energy in the form of electro-magnetic radiation having a wide range of frequencies. The Earth intercepts a mere beam of solar radiation, and although a large part of this is reflected from the Earth, especially from clouds, that fraction of the solar beam which does arrive at the Earth's surface supplies all life on Earth with its needs. These needs are closely associated with the circulation of the atmosphere.

A characteristic feature of energy is that any of its variety of forms, such as heat, light, electrical, chemical, may readily be converted into any other form. Part of the solar radiation which arrives at the Earth is converted into heat energy. Some of this is absorbed by the atmosphere and some by the waters of the ocean.

Solar radiation, as stated above, comprises a wide range of frequencies. Some 52 per cent of the total range come within the optical frequency band of electro-magnetic radiation. This forms the visible part of insolation. About six per cent of solar radiation have frequencies higher than optical frequencies. These form ultra-violet radiation, most of which is absorbed at a very high altitude above the tropopause. The remaining 42 per cent of solar radiation arriving at the Earth form infra-red radiation having frequencies lower than optical frequencies. The atmosphere allows this part of insolation to pass through it without affecting it, the air being said to be transparent to infra-red radiation. This radiation is partly absorbed by ocean waters to a relatively great depth, and partly by the Earth's land surface which is penetrated to a depth of not more than a couple of inches or so. The ocean waters and continental land, having been warmed by solar radiation, themselves become radiators which emit relatively low-frequency radiation which the atmosphere is able to absorb. The air in the troposphere, therefore, is heated essentially from below. Convective processes, stemming from this heating, are confined to the troposphere.

It has been found that the average temperature of the Earth's surface, as a whole, has remained constant for a very long period of time. It follows, therefore, that an energy balance exists between that which is received from the Sun and that which the Earth herself emits into space. If such a balance did not exist the Earth would continually be getting warmer or colder, and this is found not to be the case.

Now although an energy balance or heat balance applies to the Earth as a whole, the relative amounts of incoming and outgoing radiation are different for different latitudes. The equatorial region receives more radiation than do polar regions, this being due to the spherical shape of the Earth which results in the angle of incidence of the Sun's rays being greater in equatorial regions than in polar regions. It has been demonstrated that the equatorial zone of the Earth, bounded by the parallels of latitude 30° N. and 30° S., receives more radiation than it emits, and that the remaining parts of the Earth emit more radiation than they receive. It may be thought, therefore, that the equatorial region of the Earth is progressively getting warmer and that the polar regions are progressively getting colder. This, however, is not the case, the imbalance being offset by a meridianal transport of heat from the equatorial zone to each of the polar caps. This transport of heat energy takes place in the atmosphere and in the ocean by virtue of the circulations of these fluids.

We have noted above that water-vapour in the atmosphere plays an important role in respect of weather. It is through the agency of the water-vapour content of the air that energy is transported polewards by the atmosphere from equatorial regions.

Whenever air is in contact with a water-body there takes place a continual process whereby liquid water changes into water-vapour, this being transferred to the air, at the same time as water-vapour changes into liquid water, this being transferred to the water-body. A balance in this two-way process exists only when the air is saturated with water-vapour. If the air is not saturated with water-vapour the rate of evaporation of water exceeds that of the condensation of water-vapour. In the changing of state from vapour to liquid, or vice versa, energy is required. This energy is in the form of latent heat. Latent heat is released to the atmosphere whenever condensation of atmospheric water-vapour takes place. Conversely, latent heat is absorbed from the atmosphere whenever evaporation takes place. Evaporation, therefore, gives rise to cooling, whereas condensation brings about a warming effect on the air. Similarly, when liquid-water changes into ice, or vice versa, energy in the form of latent heat is used. When ice melts heat is released to the water which forms, and when ice forms heat is extracted from the water which surrounds the newly-formed ice.

The latent heat of water exceeds that of all other common liquids; so that when ice melts or when water freezes, or when water-vapour condenses or when liquid water evaporates, relatively large quantities of energy are released or absorbed. Since water is universally available on the Earth, especially in oceanic regions, the energy changes which take place in the atmosphere, on account of water changing from one to another of its three states, are of great importance in respect of weather. The ability of the atmosphere to evaporate water is partly dependent upon the air temperature. The higher is the air temperature the greater is the proportion of water-vapour, compared with the permanent atmospheric gases, capable of being accommodated in the air. This means that if air which is saturated with water-vapour is cooled, condensation will probably take place. On the other hand, if saturated air is warmed it will cease to be saturated and evaporation will proceed provided that water is available.

The heating of the atmosphere is greatest in equatorial regions where the Sun's rays strike the surface more vertically than in other regions. As a result of heating, the density of the air at the surface decreases and upward motion is eventually initiated. Over the ocean active evaporation continues so long as the air is not saturated. In equatorial regions warm, moist air at the surface is displaced upwards to be replaced by cooler and relatively dry air from higher levels, so that evaporation continues and humid air is constantly being carried upwards by convective processes.

The air over the ground in equatorial regions has a high water-vapour content. The cooling resulting from expansion as this air rises causes condensation of water-vapour at levels about 2000 feet above the sea surface. This gives rise to the large amount of dense cumulus cloud which is characteristic of the generally overcast oceanic equatorial belt

The warming of surface air in equatorial regions, and its subsequent upward displacement, results in relatively low atmospheric pressure at the sea surface. This initiates an air circulation in the vertical plane, in which air blows along the surface towards the

Equator to replace that which has moved upwards. At high levels air in this vertical circulation moves polewards.

Because of the Earth's rotation, moving air in the northern hemisphere is continually dragged to the right of the direction of its motion by an apparent deflecting force named after Gustave de Coriolis, a French physicist of the 19th century, who first explained it. In the southern hemisphere the so-called coriolis force acts to the left of the direction of motion of a moving air mass.

The air moving polewards at high levels from the equatorial belt loses heat-energy. It therefore cools this leading to an increase in its density which, in turn, causes it to descend. Branches of this descending air, on reaching the surface in the vicinity of 30° N., and in 30° S., flow equatorwards to form the trade-winds. Because of coriolis force the trade-winds blow from the North-east quarter in the northern hemisphere and from the South-east quarter in the southern hemisphere. The trade-wind takes its name, on account of its steadiness in direction, from the Greek word *tradus*, meaning 'track'.

The zone along which the north-east and south-east trade-winds meet is the cloudy region, described above, in which winds are generally light and rainstorms and squalls frequent. The zones which mark the poleward limits of the trades are, like the equatorial belt, regions of light variable winds. But barometric pressure in these regions of descending air tends to be high. Air humidity here is relatively low and the skies tend to be cloudless. These are the sub-tropical high-pressure zones which, over the land-surfaces of the globe, are the hottest regions on Earth.

The sub-tropical high-pressure belts are regions of outblowing winds. On the equatorial sides are to be found the trade-winds. On the poleward sides, because of coriolis force, the winds have a westerly component, for which reason the zones on the poleward sides of the sub-tropical high-pressure regions, extending polewards to the vicinity of the 60th parallels of latitude, are called the westerlies.

The zones along the poleward limit of the westerlies are regions of relatively low pressure where relatively warm, moist air is forced to rise above the cold, and therefore dense, air which flows equatorwards from the ice-covered polar regions where atmospheric pressure at sea-level is relatively high.

The wind-belts we have described above would be well-marked features of atmospheric circulation were the Earth completely covered with water. The distribution of the continental landmasses however, has a marked effect on the wind circulation. During summertime air pressure at sea-level over the continents tends to be lower than that over the oceans in similar latitudes. The reverse applies in wintertime.

Because the southern continent is predominantly sea-covered—the continents tapering southwards—the pressure and wind patterns in this hemisphere follow closely the belted structure we have described for a completely sea-covered Earth. In the northern hemisphere, however, where continental land-masses are comparable in area with that of the adjacent ocean, the belted structure gives way to a quasi-circular pattern of pressure and wind systems.

2. General Climate of the Atlantic

A zone of low-pressure cells is to be found in the Atlantic, the east-west axis of which corresponds to the so-called thermal equator. The thermal equator is the line on the Earth on which average air temperatures are greatest. This line migrates seasonally with the changing declination of the Sun.

The temperature of the surface water in the southern hemisphere is, in general, lower than that in the northern hemisphere. This follows because of the small ratio between the land and sea areas in the southern hemisphere. The thermal equator, therefore, lies to the north of the geographical equator. During northern winter it lies only slightly to the north of the geographical equator in the Atlantic, but during the summer month of July, when it lies furthest from the geographical equator, the thermal equator lies approximately along the parallel of latitude 5° N.

The air isotherms on a hypothetical Earth completely covered with water would tend to lie along parallels of latitude. The effect of the southward tapering continents however, is for the isotherms to bend polewards over continents in equatorial and middle-latitude regions, and equatorwards in these regions over the oceans. The degree of curvature of the air isotherms is most pronounced near the Equator. In any latitude where water predominates the curvature is slight, and this applies generally to the southern hemisphere. In high northern latitudes the effect of the continents results in the air isotherms tending to trend in the reverse direction to that in equatorial regions. In other words the isotherms tend to bend polewards in high north latitudes in the Atlantic.

The changing declination of the Sun modifies the pattern of isotherms described above. In the southern hemisphere during southern winter the cooling of the relatively small land-masses has only a slight effect on the air temperature and hence on the pattern of isotherms. In the northern hemisphere, on the other hand, the cooling of the relatively large land-masses during northern winter has a marked effect on air temperature. The effect is enhanced by the oceanic circulation of the North Atlantic surface waters in which warm, north-flowing currents are found on the western side and cool south-flowing currents are found on the eastern side.

The effect of the easterly trade-winds and the west-flowing ocean currents in equatorial regions causes the western parts of the Atlantic in the trade-wind belts in both hemispheres to be warmer than the eastern parts. On the poleward sides of the sub-tropical high-pressure systems the prevailing westerly winds and easterly ocean currents cause the eastern parts of the Atlantic in the regions of the westerlies in both hemispheres to be warmer than the western parts in these regions.

In the North Atlantic the high-pressure cell centred in the sub-tropical zone is called the Azores High: this zone embraces the so-called Horse Latitudes in the North Atlantic. To the north of the westerlies high-pressure belt the low-pressure cell centred in the North Atlantic is called the Iceland Low. These two cells are well-defined pressure systems, the Azores High being particularly well-developed during northern summer, and the Iceland Low being prominent during northern winter.

The air-pressure systems and their associated wind patterns migrate seasonally, like the thermal equator, with the changing declination of the Sun. There is a time-lag however, between the changing declination of the Sun and the migrating wind belts. In the case of the trade-winds, which are more pronounced on the eastern side of the North and South Atlantic, the seasonal latitudinal range is about 10°. In the North Atlantic the north-east trade-wind can be picked up by ships travelling southwards from North-West Europe in about latitude 36° N., which is the latitude of the Strait of Gibraltar.

The average northern limit of the north-east trade-wind is about 27° N., although in the eastern part of the North Atlantic the average limit is about 33° N. In the South Atlantic the average southern limit is about 35° S., which is the latitude of Cape Town. The equatorial limits of the north-east trade-wind vary from about 13° N. in August to 2° N. in February. Those of the south-east trade-wind vary between 12° S. and 1° S. for the same two months.

The Atlantic trade-winds are strongest when the Sun is in the opposite hemisphere and is at its maximum declination. At this time of the year the north-east trade-wind blows more northerly and the south-east trade more southerly than at other times. When the Sun is in the same hemisphere the trades are weakest and they tend to blow more easterly.

The equatorial region lying between the trade-wind belts is known as the doldrums. It was in the doldrums that sailing-ships were often becalmed for days, and sometimes weeks, at a time. This region has its least average width, about 100 miles, during February. In August the width of the doldrums is greatest, being about 300 miles. Sometimes the trades from opposite hemispheres meet in the vicinity of the meridian of 30° W. This was the normal position sailing-ship masters made for, where, on occasions, they were sometimes fortunate to pass from one trade to the other in a mere squall. The most favourable time of the year for crossing the doldrums in a sailing-vessel was between December and June.

During northern summer the north-east trade-wind crosses the Equator to become north-westerly. On the eastern side of the Atlantic the trade-winds carry relatively cool air equatorwards. This air becomes increasingly more humid and warmer, and convection currents within it give rise to broken cumulus clouds which are characteristic of the trade-winds region, especially on the eastern side of the Atlantic. Other weather features of the trade-wind belts are clear weather with excellent visibility and relatively little rain. The average wind speed of the north-east trade is about 10 knots, but that of the south-east trade, where the fetch is greater than it is in the North Atlantic, is about 15 knots.

Off the west coast of Africa in the vicinity of Morocco in the northern, and South-west Africa, in the southern hemisphere, the trade-winds blow roughly parallel to the coast. This gives rise to upwelling of cold oceanic water which chills the air, and which often gives rise to widespread, thick cloud-banks and sometimes fog.

Along the west coast of South Africa and in the Gulf of Guinea as far north as Cape Palmas, south-westerly winds prevail between June and September, these representing a monsoon effect resulting from the intense low atmospheric pressure in the Saharan region of North Africa. These onshore winds bring considerable rain to coastal regions in this vicinity.

Between Cape Verde and Cape Lopez, near the Equator in the Gulf of Guinea, a dry easterly wind of moderate force called the Harmattan, blows in northern winter. This brings about hazy weather due to the large quantities of fine Saharan sand which is borne aloft by the strong breeze.

In Central American waters the prevailing wind is easterly. This, however, is subject to land and sea breezes which, in the islands of the Greater Antilles, never fail and where they are stronger than anywhere else on the globe.

The phenomenon known as land and sea breezes stems from the differential heating of land and the adjacent sea. This results in relatively low pressure over the land, giving rise to a sea breeze during the daytime, and relatively low pressure over the sea giving rise to a land breeze during the night.

In the coastal waters of Venezuela the predominant easterly wind is often known by the Dutch name *Passaat* (trade-wind).

In the Mexican Gulf the trade-wind prevails from March to September, but during northern winter the high pressure over the cold North American continent gives rise to cold outblowing winds which often bring bitterly cold, and sometimes frosty, weather to the sea areas off the coasts of Texas and Louisiana. These cold, northerly winds are known locally as Northers.

In the Florida Strait and over the Bahamas the regular trade-wind is interrupted by Northers during wintertime. The trade-wind in these areas normally blows a little to the north of east in winter, and a little to the south of east in summer.

In the Atlantic, to the east of that part of the South American coast stretching from Cape San Rocque to Bahia in Brazil, the south-east trade-wind prevails, blowing east-south-east from September to March, but from a more southerly direction during the rest of the year. Between Bahia and Rio de Janeiro, from September to February, the prevailing wind blows north-north-east to east, being strongest in December. This arises from a monsoon effect caused by the intense low pressure which builds up in southern summer in the Amazon Basin. During southern summer the wind in this vicinity is usually south-east. Land and sea breezes are felt along the whole of the Brazilian coastlands.

Between Rio de Janeiro and the estuary of the River Plate, north-easterly winds prevail from October to April, and south-westerly winds from May to September.

Southwards of the River Plate the prevailing wind is westerly during the whole of the year. In the Drake Passage westerly gales succeed each other in quick succession during the greater part of the year, although, during the period April to June, fine weather is experienced and easterly winds are not uncommon.

On the eastern side of the South Atlantic the prevailing wind is south-east.

In the southern hemisphere the westerlies cover a zone between the 35th and 60th parallels. This belt of strong winds is known to seamen as the Roaring Forties.

In the westerlies belt of the North Atlantic the cold easterly winds from the polar regions to the north meet the warm, moist westerly winds of middle latitudes. It is along this zone of converging winds, a zone known as the polar front, that the travelling depressions of middle latitudes form. A similar polar front exists in the South Atlantic.

Along the North Atlantic polar front the warmer and moister air on the equatorial side rises over the colder and drier air to the north. Condensation within the warm, moist air gives rise to a thick belt of cloud with much precipitation associated with the polar front.

The prevailing winds on the western side of the Atlantic in both hemispheres are relatively dry on account of their continental origin. It follows that precipitation is less pronounced on the western side of the Atlantic in the westerlies belt than on the eastern side where the winds have an oceanic origin.

With the seasonal change in the Sun's declination the rainbelts forming the doldrums and westerlies migrate latitudinally. The characteristic features of the climate of the regions on the eastern side of ocean basins between the parallels of about 30° and 40° N. and S., are winter rain, which falls when the region comes under the influence of the westerlies; and summer drought, which is experienced when the region falls under the influence of the continental trade-winds. This type of climate is called mediterranean because the classical Mediterranean region, amongst others, experiences it.

Poor visibility over the sea is generally caused by condensation of water-vapour which results when warm, moist air comes into contact with sea-water at a lower temperature. Condensation of water-vapour can occur only when so-called condensation nuclei are present in the air. These nuclei are always present to a greater or lesser degree, in the atmosphere. Fog is not common over the oceans in tropical and sub-tropical regions.

The most fog-bound region of the Atlantic Ocean is in the vicinity of the Grand Banks of Newfoundland. In this region the warm and moist southerly winds of spring and summer, having been warmed in passing over the Gulf Stream waters of the western North Atlantic, are chilled on coming into contact with the cold, often ice-laden, waters of the Labrador current, which cover the Grand Banks region. The type of fog which forms in this locality is called sea-fog or advection fog.

During winter the winds in the Grand Banks region are usually westerly and, having originated over the North American continent, they are relatively dry. The frequency of fog during winter is, therefore, lower than in summer in the Grand Banks area. A shift of wind in this locality from west to south-west during clear weather is a sure indication of fog. On the other hand, in thick weather a shift of wind from west to north-west usually brings clear weather.

Fog is not uncommon off the so-called cold-water coasts of Morocco and South-west Africa on account of upwelling of cold oceanic waters.

3. *Atlantic Hurricanes*

The weather of the trade-wind belts is characterised by regularity: yet within parts of these belts, storms of exceptional violence, in which atmospheric pressure is extremely low and winds blow with great force, often occur. These violent atmospheric disturbances are called tropical storms which, in the Atlantic, are known as hurricanes. The word *hurricane* comes from the language of the ancient Caribs of Amerindia and means 'great wind'.

The hurricane is essentially a phenomenon of the ocean, and fortunately relatively few reach far inland. Those which do travel across the land tend to fill in quickly but in the process of doing so they often have devastating effects on human life and property.

Atlantic hurricanes tend to swing clockwise around the periphery of the sub-tropical high-pressure system of the North Atlantic—the Azores High. The characteristic path of a hurricane, therefore, is westwards in its initial stages of development and then polewards as a fully-developed storm. The westward motion changes to northerly at a position called the point of re-curvature of the storm, but occasionally the westward motion is maintained and the hurricane passes on to the United States mainland or across West Indian islands. Fortunately hurricanes travel at the relatively slow speed of between about 15 and 20 knots: so that, if warning of a hurricane's approach is given, some preparation may be made to reduce the risk to human life and to prevent undue loss or damage to property.

Atlantic hurricanes occur most frequently during late summer and early autumn. They rarely occur as early as June and seldom after September. The hurricane season in the West Indies is often remembered from the rhyme:

> June too soon,
> July stand by,
> August look out you must,
> September remember,
> October all over.

D

With the assistance of radar a ship's captain is often able to obtain confirmation that a hurricane is in the vicinity. On a radar-scope the picture of a tropical storm appears as a spiral pattern of densely-packed echoes which are reflected from the heavy precipitation around the central low pressure of the storm.

Hurricanes, the worst of all atmospheric storms, are capable of causing great devastation, the energy of such a storm exceeding that of any other natural terrestrial phenomenon.

On a weather-chart a hurricane appears as a compact system of tightly-spaced isobars in which the pressure gradient between the centre and the periphery is very great, the atmospheric pressure at the centre being abnormally low. Windspeeds within the system often exceed 100 knots; rain is torrential and is accompanied by thunder and lightning; and seas are mountainous. In its initial developing stage a hurricane has a relatively small diameter in the order of tens of miles. When fully developed its diameter rarely exceeds 300 or 400 miles, so that hurricanes are more confined than the low-pressure systems of middle latitudes.

Most Atlantic hurricanes commence their turbulent careers in the region to the south-east of the Bahamas in a zone of latitude between about 8° and 20° N. During late summer and early autumn in the northern hemisphere this zone is occupied by the doldrums. At this time of year the sea temperature here is at its maximum and the doldrums lie furthest removed from the Equator in a sufficiently high latitude for coriolis force to initiate a whirling motion to moving air. The South Atlantic is free from hurricanes, the reason being that the doldrums in the Atlantic never pass to the southwards of the Equator.

Local heating of air causes a reduction in pressure, this leading to an upward motion of warm, moist air which is given a spiral motion by coriolis force arising from the Earth's rotation. The rising air is replaced by cooler air at the surface which circulates in an anti-clockwise direction. The rising air is cooled to a temperature below its dew point and condensation of water-vapour leads to the development of cloud and rain. In the process of condensation liberated latent heat warms the air the upward motion of which is consequently accelerated.

In the absence of radar, seamen may recognise the approach of a hurricane from well-known precursory signs. Included amongst these are the extensive cover of cirrus cloud, which gives rise to lurid sunsets and dawns; and the heavy swell which moves outwards from, and more quickly than, the storm system. A skilful captain, recognising the approach of a hurricane, would normally take steps to avoid being caught in the storm area, particularly that part of the advancing half in which there is a directional component of the wind towards the path of the storm. In this part of the storm area, which is known as the dangerous quadrant, the wind-strength is greater than in any other part of the storm. If the storm area cannot be avoided the captain aims to ascertain his ship's position relative to the storm's centre, and to place his vessel in the safest attitude. This may be done from wind and barometer observations. If the wind shifts clockwise, that is to say, if the wind veers, and the air pressure falls, the observer lies within the dangerous quadrant. On the other hand if, with a falling barometer, the wind backs, or shifts anti-clockwise, the observer lies in the so-called navigable quadrant, in which the wind tends to blow in a direction away from the path of the storm.

In bygone days, before the advent of radio, sailing-ship captains were forced to rely on their own weather observations for detecting the approach of a tropical storm. Nowadays navigators are often able to obtain advance warning of the positions and movements of hurricanes by radio signals transmitted from the United States Weather Bureau. A special department of this bureau, centred at Miami in Florida, is concerned specifically with hurricane observations and forecasts, and in this connection organised weather flights are undertaken from air bases in Bermuda, Florida and Puerto Rico. On receipt of a hurricane report from a ship at sea a specially-equipped aircraft is flown to the storm area in order to obtain meteorological observations of temperature, pressure and humidity, so that the probable path of the storm may be assessed, and warning to shore folk, as well as to seamen, may be given as quickly as possible. Appropriately enough hurricanes are given female names for identification purposes. The first of the season is given a name, such as Alma, which begins with the letter A; the second is given a name beginning with B, such as Bertha, and so on.

Associated with hurricanes are devastating sea-waves of abnormal amplitude which often flood large areas of coastland resulting in extensive damage to crops and property, and often in loss of life. This provides justification for the large sums of money devoted to the forecasting of storm-paths, so that timely warnings may be given.

The exceptionally low atmospheric pressure at the centre of a hurricane gives rise to a considerable variation in sea-level within the storm area. As the storm moves across the ocean, oscillations of the sea surface are initiated, these resulting in the heavy swell to be observed in sea areas far removed from the storm centre.

An atmospheric disturbance of great intensity similar to, but confined to a very much more restricted area than, a tropical storm, is the tornado. Winds in tornadoes, known in the United States as twisters, have speeds greater than those in hurricanes, often exceeding 200 knots. Tornadoes are short-lived and seldom last for more than an hour or so. Their diameters do not usually exceed 500 yards, and they travel at speeds of about 20 knots. They are most frequent in the Mississippi Valley where they often cause great destruction and loss of life.

The familiar characteristic feature of a tornado is its funnel-like pendant cloud which hangs from a dense cloud-bank aloft. The cloud is formed by condensation of water-vapour due to cooling resulting from the abnormally low pressure within the vortex.

Tornadoes which pass from land to sea become violent water-spouts. These are not to be confused with the fair-weather water-spout which has an origin different from that of a tornado. This harmless phenomenon is due to air of high humidity at a locally-warm surface by virtue of which a rotating column of ascending air is initiated. Cooling results in condensation and the formation of a tube of cloud which often leads to the production of a large cumulus cloud at its top.

PART I

CHAPTER 4

ATLANTIC WATER MOVEMENTS

1. Introduction

The waters of the hydrosphere are in perpetual motion. The movement of the ocean, which is exceedingly complex, is studied in relation to waves, currents, tides and tidal streams. Let us investigate each of these phenomena in turn, with particular reference to the Atlantic.

2. Atlantic Waves

It is seldom that the sea surface is smooth and level. Even in a perfect calm, when the sea surface is glassy, the ocean waters usually heave up and down with small or large amplitude. The undulations of the sea, which are normally due to the wind, are called waves or swell. Sea-waves are the immediate result of local wind, whereas swells are the repercussions due to wind-action elsewhere.

An interesting feature of sea-waves and swell is their quick movement across the sea surface. At first sight it would appear that the water itself is moving in the direction of the waves, but this is not the case. The water in which waves move does not possess translatory motion except perhaps to a small degree. Each particle of water affected by waves merely moves more or less vertically upwards and downwards as each wave passes.

Every wave possesses a crest and a trough, the vertical distance between which being the wave height. The distance between the crest of a wave and the following trough, measured in the direction of the wave propagation, is half the wave length. During the passage of crest, trough and succeeding crest, that is to say, during the time in which the wave form moves through one wave length, each particle of water at the surface moves upwards and downwards through a vertical distance equal to the wave height. The interval of time during which this happens is called the period of the wave.

When wind develops after a calm over a glassy sea, the first waves to appear have wave lengths of no more than a few centimetres. These tiny wavelets, which are known as capillary waves, are a response to surface tension of the water and friction between the moving air and the sea. As the windspeed increases capillary waves transform into waves of increased height and length, known as gravity waves. These move away from the source region conveying energy derived from the wind.

Waves continue to grow in length and height so long as the wind feeds energy to the sea more rapidly than the wind-fed energy of the waves can be dissipated. The energy of waves is a function of wave height, wave length and wave period. As wind energy is fed to the sea during the growth of waves both the height and the length of the waves increase, the growth developing in stages. As capillary waves grow in length and height new capillary waves are formed, and these pass through a transitional stage in a manner similar to that of preceding generations of waves.

The period of a wave is dependent mainly upon its length, so that waves of different lengths have different speeds. It follows that waves of different generations and different dimensions continually combine and recombine, as their phase relationships change, to produce a constantly changing pattern of undulations. The seemingly confused pattern of waves normally to be seen when the sea is rough is a mixture of numerous wave trains, and it is by no means an easy task to separate or distinguish the individual wave components.

The dimensions of waves in deep water depend upon the strength of the wind, the time during which the wind has been blowing, and the direction of the wind, especially in relation to the extent of sea, or fetch as it is called, lying to leeward of the source region.

In the Southern Ocean, where the wind often blows steadily and persistently from the west with considerable force, the great extent of the fetch gives rise to waves of large dimensions. In the stormy North Atlantic the fetch of the wind blowing in an intense extra-tropical storm seldom exceeds a few hundred miles, and it is rare, therefore, for wave heights here to exceed about 50 feet. In the majority of severe Atlantic storms the waves usually have heights of less than about 30 feet. The lengths of North Atlantic storm-waves are about 500 feet, but in the Southern Ocean lengths of 1200 feet are not uncommon.

The confused, irregular pattern of waves normally to be observed in the ocean is called sea. Sea is described as calm, light, moderate, heavy or mountainous, with increasing wave height. Sea is usually accompanied by white caps and broken water from crests and from the whipping up of spray.

When waves pass out of their source region they normally lose height and increase their length as they are transformed into swell. Swells normally have considerably greater lengths than do storm-waves, and in the North Atlantic swells having lengths of between 2000 and 3000 feet are not uncommon.

From a mathematical consideration of sea-waves in deep water, the length of a sea-wave is proportional to the square of its period, and the speed of travel is proportional to the wave length of the wave. From these relationships a wave having a period of four seconds has a length of about 80 feet and a speed of about 20 feet per second. The length and speed of a wave whose period is 16 seconds are 1300 feet and 80 feet per second approximately.

In a North Atlantic storm the wind blows almost along the isobars, so that with a wind increasing in force the waves run initially approximately along the isobars, thereafter tending to travel along great-circle tracks. A shift of wind, due to the storm movement, results in a new wave train developing. These, of course, interfere with their predecessors and with those which follow them.

Waves are influenced by any translatory motion of the water, such as tidal stream or current, through which they pass. Waves which travel through water which moves in a direction opposite to that of the waves tend to increase in height and to decrease in length. This causes an increase in the so-called steepness—defined as the ratio between wave height and wave length—of the waves. The greater the velocity of the moving water the greater will be the effect on the height and length of the waves. Waves which travel through water which moves in the same direction as that of the waves suffer a reduction in their steepness.

The rising and falling motion of the water through which waves pass is confined to a depth which approximates to the wave length of the waves. Below the level at this depth waves have no effect. Submarines, therefore, on meeting bad weather on the surface have merely to submerge to a relatively shallow depth to gain steadiness and comfort.

Waves are often subdued by rain or other form of precipitation, and the rough surface of the sea is often flattened by heavy rain or by a hail shower. Pack-ice has the effect of preventing waves from forming, and when the sea begins to freeze the change of state has a remarkable effect in smoothing the sea surface.

When waves approach a shelving shore their rate of travel changes. In deep water this rate is proportional to the square root of the length, but in shallow water it is proportional to the square root of the depth. In deep water sea-waves are described as free waves. This means that there is no appreciable lateral movement of the water in which the waves are moving. In shallowing water the energy of the waves becomes concentrated into a water layer of diminishing thickness.   This leads to a concentration of wave energy into a reduced volume of water, the wave height increasing and the wave length decreasing to accommodate the concentrated wave energy.   A stage is reached when a wave approaching a shelving shore changes from a free wave to a wave of translation in which water in the crests is forced forwards to form breakers and surf. The final uprush of surf, or swash, on to a shore is followed by back-wash resulting from the force of gravity asserting itself.

Much of the energy of waves which break on shores is used in destroying the land.   Almost all shores are subjected to the devastat-ing onslaught of waves.   Storm-waves are sufficiently powerful to tear away not only huge blocks of rocks from cliff faces, but also immense harbour structures, such as breakwaters and sea defences. The spectacular coastal features, such as bays, headlands, cliffs, sea-stacks and sea-caves, all bear witness to the destructive work of sea-waves.

The most destructive of all sea-waves are not generated by the wind.   They are the so-called tidal waves or *tsunamis*, which are due, not to tidal forces as their name may suggest, but to oceanic seismic activity.   Submarine earthquakes or volcanic activity on the sea-bed generate sea-waves which sweep outwards from the focal point of activity at rates amounting to 300 or 400 knots.

In the open ocean *tsunamis* pass unnoticed because of the very low ratio between their heights and lengths.   On approaching a shelving shore, however, a *tsunami* wave grows into a mountainous mass of water which strikes the shore with devastating effect, often flooding enormous areas of coastland and sometimes drowning thousands of people with little or no warning.

The tidal wave associated with the notorious Lisbon earthquake of 1755 is perhaps the most renowned of Atlantic tsunamis.   This tidal wave caused severe flooding of the Cadiz coastal area when a wave of some 50 feet higher than High Water level swamped the shore, causing havoc and destruction.

Another type of sea-wave which is often responsible for the flooding of coastlands is the storm surge or storm tide.   Storm tides are most common in the Atlantic in the hurricane area, especially in the Gulf of Mexico and along the eastern seaboard of the United States.   The strong winds within a storm area may cause water to be piled up locally, at the same time as a rise in sea-level occurs as a result of low atmospheric pressure near the storm centre.   If the storm centre moves at the same rate as that of the oscillation set up by the effects of wind and low pressure, that is to say, if a state of synchronism or resonance occurs, a storm surge may cause a wave of exceptionally great height which may bring about extensive flooding in coastal areas. The city of Galveston and its neighbourhood has suffered on more than one occasion the terrible calamity of severe flooding due to storm surges.

The most notable example of a serious storm surge affecting North-west Europe was that of 1953, when persistent and strong northerly winds caused water to pile up in the southern part of the North Sea at a time which coincided with spring tides. The sea-level rose quickly to a height many feet in excess of that predicted and large areas of the Netherlands and Eastern England were flooded. The high waves generated by the gale-force winds at the time added to the destructive capacity of the storm surge.

Atlantic Ocean sailing directions have long drawn the attention of mariners to waves called rollers which are prevalent on the Guiana coast of South America from December to March; the Virgin Islands and island groups north-west of Guadeloupe from October to March; the Cape Verde Islands from July to September; and Ascension and St. Helena at all times of the year but especially during January.

Rollers are wind-generated waves related to relatively rapid changes in atmospheric pressure over certain oceanic regions. Rollers affecting a given area are often due to swiftly-moving low-pressure systems thousands of miles away. Swell approaching a shore often results in high and steep waves which pound the shore regularly, and often persistently, making boat landings and other shipping activities hazardous.

The African coast to the south of Gibraltar has no natural harbour to protect shipping for about 500 miles. This coastal stretch is particularly prone to ground-swell, which often is a danger to ships working cargo in open roadsteads in unprotected anchorages.

3. Atlantic Currents

The waters of the hydrosphere are circulated mainly by the permanent current systems of the ocean.

Soon after seamen first began to voyage across the Atlantic the principal currents of this ocean were recognised and charted and used to advantage by Atlantic voyagers. In the open ocean mariners are able to detect and to estimate the set and rate of ocean currents by comparing the ship's position from the record of the ship's progress through the water with her position determined by astro-nomical observations. The accumulated observations of sea-currents in all parts of the world, particularly in the Atlantic Ocean, provided the means in the 19th century for charting ocean currents and their seasonal variations.   Prominent for his careful study and analyses of log-book records of currents, was the United States naval officer Lieutenant Matthew Fontaine Maury, whose famous book *The Physical Geography of the Sea* ran into many editions.   By using Maury's charts of ocean currents and winds, sailing-ship captains were able to shorten their ocean voyages considerably.

The first charts of ocean currents revealed circulatory patterns almost identical with those of the major wind systems of the globe. It was not unnatural, therefore, to think that the oceanic circulation was a direct consequence of atmospheric circulation.   It is now recognised that, [although the wind certainly influences the pattern of oceanic circulation, other factors have pronounced effects.] [In investigating ocean currents it is often extremely difficult to separate cause from effect,] and the close study of ocean currents poses problems the answers to which are still being investigated. [Wind certainly plays a part in initiating ocean currents, but so also may differential heating or evaporation which brings about unequal distribution of sea temperature and salinity, and thus of density. Wind influences the rate of evaporation of sea-water, so that, in addition to the main effect of wind in causing a surface current through frictional drag, a secondary effect is also present.   Freezing of sea-water and ice melting in the ocean also affect sea-water density and these factors, in turn, influence the oceanic circulation. River-water entering the sea is clearly responsible for affecting the circulation of the ocean, at least near river mouths.]

[In addition to the primary factors which initiate ocean currents, mentioned above, other secondary factors come into play as a result of the movement of the water itself.   Turbulence, for example, may initiate counter currents, or reaction currents as these are often called.   The most important of these secondary factors is due to the rotation of the Earth, which gives rise to coriolis force.   Any moving mass, such as a body of oceanic water which has been set in motion through some primary cause such as wind or density differences, tends to move in a fixed horizontal direction in space.   Because the Earth is spinning, fixed horizontal directions in space differ from those relative to the Earth's surface.   Relative to the Earth's surface all horizontally-moving bodies in the northern hemisphere tend to be dragged to the right of their lines of motion.] In the southern hemisphere they tend to be dragged to the left of their lines of motion by an apparent force, which is coriolis force.   Coriolis force is zero at the Equator, and its magnitude increases with the latitude.

[A stream of ocean water meeting an obstacle, such as a continental shore, results in a tendency for the sea surface to slope downwards from the shore. The force of gravity asserting itself on water, the surface of which is not level tends to form a hydraulic current, the energy for which being provided by the hydrostatic head due to the sea slope.

Where ocean currents meet at the surface, a downward motion of water is initiated. Such a region is called a zone of convergence. In contrast, upward motion of water is to be expected at a zone of divergence at which surface currents move in opposite directions. This serves to remind us of the fact that the circulation of the oceans is a three-dimensional circulation, not a two-dimensional phenomenon, as we may be led to believe from the familiar ocean-current charts.

Extending across the equatorial zone of the Atlantic there are two westward-flowing currents known respectively as the North and South Equatorial currents. These seem to have been initiated by the converging trade-winds which force surface waters in their vicinity towards the west. Wedged between the North and South Equatorial currents is the Equatorial counter current which flows eastwards, and is often thought of as being a compensatory flow, or hydraulic current, which assists in offsetting the upward slope of the sea surface towards the west, a slope brought about by wind-drag.

The South Equatorial current strikes the shoulder of Brazil where it splits, part swinging southwards along the Brazilian coast, and part sweeping north-eastwards to join the North Equatorial current.

The current flows westwards along the north coast of South America and through the channels and passages between the islands of the Antilles.

The piling up of water at the western end of the Caribbean gives rise to a strong hydraulic current which sweeps through the Yucatan Channel between the Yucatan Peninsula and Cuba at a rate of three or four knots. A similar hydraulic effect provides the mainspring which results in the strong stream emerging from the Gulf of Mexico through the Florida Strait between the Florida Peninsula and Cuba and thence into the open Atlantic to the north-west of the Bahamas. The Florida current tends to follow the eastern North American coastland as far north as Cape Hatteras, and large eddies on the western side are often held to have caused the long, sweeping bays of the American coast of the Carolinas, Georgia and Florida. The current in the shallow coastal waters in this vicinity runs southwards counter to the north-flowing Florida current.

The Florida current leaves the coast and heads north-eastwards into the open ocean at Cape Hatteras. From here to the vicinity of the Grand Banks of Newfoundland the current is known as the Gulf Stream.

The swift-flowing Gulf Stream hems in to the south-east the relatively sluggish waters of the Sargasso Sea, which occupies the central region of the great oceanic whirl of the North Atlantic circulation. The Sargasso Sea is renowned for its deep blue colour, an indication of a paucity of marine microscopic life in its waters.

To the east of the Grand Banks of Newfoundland the Gulf Stream loses its stream character. In this locality the water spreads out to become a shallow and comparatively slow-moving water-body in contrast to the character of the Gulf Stream proper. The configuration of the several branches formed from the Gulf Stream, which spread northwards and eastwards from the Grand Banks region, is called the North Atlantic drift.

The temperature of the waters in the North Atlantic drift is considerably lower than that of the Gulf Stream off Cape Hatteras. Cooling of these waters is due largely to the influence of the Labrador current which flows southwards to the vicinity of the mouth of the Hudson River, where its high density causes it to sink below the warmer and less dense, even though more saline, waters of the Gulf Stream.

Part of the waters of the Gulf Stream flows northwards towards Greenland where it mixes with southward-flowing cold water of the East Greenland current. The combined water-flow forms the West Greenland current which sets northwards on the east side of the Davis Strait. Another part flows north-eastwards towards Iceland, off the south-west coast of which it swings westwards to form the Irminger current which joins the East Greenland current. A third part flows eastwards where, in the vicinity of latitude 45° N., longitude 40° W., it divides. One branch swings south-eastwards to flow along the North-west European coast south of the Bay of Biscay, and thence along the North-west African coast to form the Azores and Canaries currents. This water ultimately feeds the North Equatorial current. The second branch of the division flows north-eastwards to bathe the shores of Britain and North-west Europe with relatively warm waters.

The flow of water between Scotland and the Faeroes continues along the Norwegian coast as the Norwegian current. To the north of Norway the Norwegian current branches to form the North Cape current which flows into the Barents Sea, and the Spitsbergen current which ultimately unites with the south-flowing East Greenland current.

In the Arctic Basin the surface flow is influenced by local winds and river-flow, as well as by icemelt and freezing. The East Green-land current conveys a considerable amount of ice into the open Atlantic. The melting of this ice, especially in spring and summer helps to maintain the southerly flow of cold Arctic water.

The cold and comparatively fresh water conveyed southwards by the Labrador current has a density not very much different from that of the warm, but saline, water of the Gulf Stream. Fusing of Labrador and Gulf Stream waters brings about a mixture having a density greater than that of either of the components of the mixture. An effect of this fusion is to produce a density wall, relatively narrow in horizontal extent, which separates sharply the distinctly different waters of the Labrador current to the north-west from the Gulf Stream waters to the south-east.

It is a curious fact that in the peripheral seas of the North Atlantic, especially the North Sea, the Mediterranean Sea, the Greenland and Norwegian Seas, and the Davis Strait, the horizontal circulation is anti-clockwise in contrast to the general oceanic cir-culation of the North Atlantic which, as we have seen, is clockwise. In the South Atlantic the general circulation is anti-clockwise.

A branch of the South Equatorial current flows along the east coast of South America as the warm Brazil current. In the vicinity of latitude 40° S. the Brazil current leaves the coast, swinging east-wards towards South Africa to form the northern part of the general east-flowing current of the Southern Ocean. Part of this east-flowing stream, on meeting the South-west African coast, swings northwards to form the Benguela current which ultimately links with the South Equatorial current. The Equatorial counter current flows eastwards into the Gulf of Guinea where it is known as the Guinea current.

The Southern Ocean current, which flows eastwards in the direction of the prevailing westerly wind, on emerging from the relatively narrow Drake Passage, sends an offshoot northwards along the South American coast to flow between the mainland and the Falkland Islands as the Falkland current. This swings eastwards to the north of the Falklands to combine with the east-flowing current of the South Atlantic.

Oceanic currents have speeds which generally are less than about 10 or 12 miles per day. Exceptions occur in respect of the clearly-defined currents, such as the Florida current and the Gulf Stream. The strongest currents in the Atlantic are found on the western side, particularly in the North Atlantic where the Florida current attains speeds of five, or even more, knots. The currents on the eastern side of the Atlantic are extremely weak and their directions are greatly influenced by local changes in the wind direction.

A steady wind blowing parallel to a continental shore gives rise to a convergence or divergence, depending upon the hemisphere, and whether the shore lies to the left or right of the air-flow. At places where divergences occur, upwelling of cold oceanic water from depth gives rise to the phenomenon known as the cold-water coast.

The coast of Morocco and that of South-west Africa in the vicinity of Walvis Bay are prominent cold-water coasts of the Atlantic.

At places where steady upwelling occurs water rich in nutrients is found at the surface. In contrast, at places where downward movement of water occurs, the surface waters tend to be deficient in nutrients. Marine life, therefore, tends to be abundant in regions of upwelling and a relative paucity is common in regions where surface waters move downwards. In general cold-water coastal waters are rich fishing-grounds on account of the natural replenishment of the surface waters with nutrients brought up from greater depths.

The horizontal ocean currents discussed above are confined to a relatively thin upper layer of sea having a thickness of no more than a few hundred feet. The oceanic waters below this layer move at rates, except in certain circumstances, which are very slow.

The deep-water circulation of the oceans has been investigated closely only within recent decades, and modern techniques and instruments devised for the purpose have led to a rapid accumulation of knowledge of the ocean circulation.

Oceanographers who have studied the circulation of the Atlantic have demonstrated that the cold, dense water lying on the Atlantic floor is generated at the surface in one of two source regions, one in the South Atlantic in the Weddell Sea, and the other in the North Atlantic in the region between Iceland and Greenland.

The predominant water lying on the Atlantic floor is that which is generated in the Southern Ocean. The cold, and therefore, dense water surrounding the Antarctic continent sinks and flows downwards along the Antarctic continental shelf and slope to flood the lower parts of the Atlantic basins by way of their deep connecting channels. Antarctic bottom water, as this water is called, is to be found in the Atlantic well to the north of the Equator.

The bottom water of the North Atlantic is generated in the Irminger Sea and the Labrador Sea at localities where the warm but saline waters of the Gulf Stream intermingle with the cold waters of the Irminger and Labrador currents. Intense cooling in late autumn and winter results in the surface water sinking. On reaching the bottom this dense water spreads over the bottom of much of the North Atlantic floor. On meeting the denser Antarctic bottom water it slides over the top of the latter and continues to spread southwards across the Equator.

At the Antarctic Convergence, which lies along the vicinity of latitude 55° S., downward-moving water spreads northwards and overlies the Arctic deep and Antarctic bottom waters, forming the Antarctic intermediate water. North Atlantic intermediate water is generated at the Sub-tropical Convergence in the vicinity of latitude 35° N.

By studying and analysing temperature and salinity of samples of oceanic water from different depths, oceanographers are able to recognise the stratified structure of the ocean. A characteristic water-mass in the North Atlantic Ocean is that which is generated in the Mediterranean Sea and which flows outwards through the Gibraltar Strait along the bottom. This water is characterised by relatively high temperature and high salinity. On emerging from the Gibraltar Strait it sinks until it attains a depth at which the local water has the same density, whereupon the Mediterranean water spreads laterally, sandwiched between intermediate water above and below.

The outflow of Mediterranean water is compensated for by an inflow at the surface at the Strait of Gibraltar. The east-flowing current in the strait is initiated by the excessive evaporation within the Mediterranean Sea which is not balanced by rainfall and inflow of rivers. The vertical circulation of the Mediterranean Sea is such that the whole of the water within the Mediterranean Basin is renewed periodically with Atlantic water at intervals of about 75 years.

The Mediterranean Basin is described as a ventilated basin. In contrast, many of the fjords of the Norwegian coast are stagnant basins. The threshold at the seaward end of a fjord holds in the water below a relatively shallow depth. The surface water, which is relatively light on account of its low salinity, flows slowly seawards without mixing with water at depth. The shallowness of the entrance inhibits an inflow, so that the water which occupies low levels is deficient in oxygen and is unable, therefore, to support a flourishing fauna. If wind or an abnormally high tide results in the accumulation of dense saline water at the entrance to a fjord, an overflow of oxygen-free water over the threshold leads to a sudden ventilation of the basin and to the mass destruction of the marine life of the surface waters of the fjord.

An important consequence of oceanic circulation is the transportation of heat energy from equatorial regions to those of higher latitudes in both hemispheres. In the Atlantic the climate of temperate latitudes on the eastern side is considerably milder than that on the western side. The climate of the ice-free harbours of Norway, for example, is in striking contrast to that of the Labrador coast in the same latitude, where the harbours suffer a climatic harshness, keeping them frozen for most of the year. The so-called gulf of winter warmth which stretches far to the north in the eastern North Atlantic, is accounted for by the warming influence of the North Atlantic drift. In the South Atlantic the circulation influences the climate in that it is warmer on the western side than on the eastern side in similar latitudes. This is the result of the warm Brazil current on the western side and the colder Benguela current on the eastern side.

4. *Atlantic Tides and Tidal Streams*

The vertical oscillation of the sea-level due to so-called tidal forces is known as the tide. As a result of variations of the height of the sea-level due to the tide, horizontal water-flows, called tidal streams, are initiated. A tidal stream with which is associated a rising tide is called a flood stream, and one with which is associated a falling tide is called an ebb stream.

The rising and falling of the sea-level and the associated tidal streams must surely have been noticed by folk living on coastlands of tidal seas from earliest times, and these same folk may well have observed the connection between the workings of the tide and the changing phases of the Moon. And, indeed, from such observations, and without knowledge of the cause of the tide, it is a relatively simple matter to make reasonably good predictions of the vertical oscillations of the sea-level: and, therefore, of the times and heights of high and low waters.

The vertical distance between consecutive low- and high-water levels is called the range of the tide. Tidal ranges vary considerably from place to place. At some places the tidal range is hardly detectable, whereas at other places it may be as much as 40 feet or even more. The largest tidal range in the Atlantic occurs in the Bay of Fundy, in Canada, where it amounts to no less than 50 feet. In British waters large tidal ranges of over 40 feet occur in the Bristol Channel.

Not only do tidal ranges vary from place to place but so also do tidal rhythms. At some places the rhythm of the tide is diurnal, that is to say, each day experiences a single High Water and a single Low Water. At most places, however, two High and two Low

Waters are experienced each day, such tidal rhythms being known as semi-diurnal tides.

All tidal rhythms are the result of a combination of tidal forces, some of which tend to produce diurnal tides and others semi-diurnal tides. If the diurnal constitutents predominate at any given place the tide at that place will be diurnal in character. This happens at many places in the Gulf of Mexico, which is the only part of the Atlantic experiencing this variety of tide. At most places in the Atlantic, where semi-diurnal tidal constituents predominate, the tidal rhythm is High Water—Low Water, ever repeating every six hours or so.

The first scientist to give a rational explanation of the tide and its relationships with the apparent celestial movements of the Moon and Sun was the 18th-century English philosopher Sir Isaac Newton. Newton explained the tide in terms of his universal law of gravitation. He regarded every particle of water in the ocean as being in a state of balance under the action of the Earth's force of gravity and each of several tide-raising forces. This hypothesis formed the basis of Newton's equilibrium theory of the tide.

The principal tide-generating force is that of the Moon. The force of attraction of the Moon on the Earth and on the waters of the ocean cause the lunar tide which is a semi-diurnal tide having a period of half a lunar day, that is about $12\frac{1}{2}$ hours.

As a result of the differential forces of gravity between the Moon and the water particles lying on the Earth's surface the Earth's hydrosphere tends to form an ellipsoidal envelope, the major axis of which lies on the line joining the centres of the Moon and Earth. Were the Earth completely covered with water, and if the Moon had no declination, that is to say if the Moon were always on the plane of the Earth's equator, the Moon's tide-generating force would cause a permanent low water at each pole.

As the Earth rotates within the ellipsoidal hydrosphere the sea-level would oscillate such that a graph of the changing level of the sea against time would be a sine, or, as it is sometimes called, a harmonic curve.

The Sun produces a similar harmonic oscillation of the sea-level to that of the Moon, known as the solar tide. The amplitude of the solar tide is about three-sevenths of that of the lunar tide. The Moon, being so much nearer to the Earth than is the Sun, is the predominant tide-raising body, even though the mass of the Moon is only a tiny fraction of that of the Sun.

When the Moon is New or Full, the Moon's and Sun's tide-generating forces act conjointly, so that the combination luni-solar

E

tide has a maximum range. At the times of First and Third Quarters, when the Moon and Sun are in quadrature, the Moon's tide-generating force acts out of phase with the Sun's tide-generating force, and the range of the tide is least. Maximum tidal ranges, which should occur theoretically at the times of New and Full Moons, give rise to Spring tides. Minimum tidal ranges, which should occur at the times of First and Third Quarters, give rise to Neap tides. Springs and Neaps each occur twice during each lunation, that is once a fortnight.

The changing declinations of the Moon and the Sun produce diurnal tidal constituents and so also do the periodic changing distances between the Moon and the Earth and the Sun and the Earth.

The character of the tide is not completely described by Newton's equilibrium theory. Present-day research into tidal problems are based on dynamical principles rather than on statical principles, such as those used in Newton's equilibrium theory.

The ocean and peripheral seas may be regarded as forming a number of natural basins in which the sea oscillates in response to certain tidal forces. If the tidal forces have a resultant period or frequency equivalent to that of the natural period or frequency of the water-body within the basin, the latter frequency depending upon the size and configuration of the basin, a state of synchronism or resonance will occur and this will cause the oscillations to be very pronounced.

The fact that the Earth is spinning slowly on its axis gives rise to a rotatory motion of the horizontally-moving waters in a tidal system, or amphidromic system, as it is called. In an amphidromic system lines radiating from a point, known as an amphidromic point, link places at which the time of High Water is the same. An amphidromic point is the centre of a system of quasi-circular lines joining places at which the tidal range is the same. At an amphidromic point the tidal range is zero, and as distance from such a point increases within the system, so does the tidal range.

The large semi-diurnal tides of the North Atlantic coastal areas are regarded as being due to a large amphidromic system centred in the North Atlantic roughly midway between the British Isles and Newfoundland.

The North Sea, the tidal features of which have been studied intensively, comprises at least three amphidromic systems.

In the open ocean tidal streams are relatively weak. But oceanic tidal streams approaching shallow coastal waters set these waters oscillating, and where resonance occurs vigorous tidal movements result. Tidal streams in many narrow coastal channels often attain rates of 10 knots or more.

An unusual and dramatic effect of the tide is the tidal bore. When a tidal stream flows into an estuary the restricting effect of the narrowing and shallowing estuary causes a distortion of the tidal rhythm, such that the interval between Low Water and the following High Water is progressively shortened, and that between High Water and the following Low Water lengthened, with increasing distance upstream. In extreme cases the flood stream flows upriver with an almost vertical wavefront to form a tidal bore. Well-known tidal bores of North-west Europe are those of the Seine, Severn and Trent. The bore of the Amazon of South America is remarkable in respect of the great distance, some 200 miles, of its travel upstream.

The tide allows deep-draughted ships to negotiate normally shallow channels and rivers at or near the time of High Water. At seaports where tidal ranges are more than about 10 feet it is necessary to arrange for enclosed docks, or floating harbours as they are sometimes called, to allow ships to remain afloat at all stages of the tide. Entrance to a floating harbour, the water of which is kept at a constant level, is by way of a lock fitted with two lock-gates, the inner one impounding the water in the floating harbour.

5. Ice in the Atlantic

The most extensive ice cover of the northern hemisphere is the ice crust which almost covers the Arctic Ocean. During the summer, when this immense raft of ice has its least extent, its area is about four times that of the Greenland ice-cap.

The striking feature of the polar sea-ice is the remarkable effect of the North Atlantic drift, the warm waters of which bite into the Arctic ice for hundreds of miles in the Barents Sea and the waters to the north of Norway. The least accessible part of the polar ice in the northern hemisphere lies some 350 miles from the geographical pole in the vicinity of latitude 84° N., longitude 175° W.

In winter the polar ice increases in thickness largely by growth on its submerged face. Ice in the Arctic Ocean has a thickness, due to normal growth from freezing, of seldom more than about five feet, although, in the case of floe-ice several years old, the thickness may be as much as 14 feet. Greater thicknesses than this are possible through a process known as rafting or hummocking, whereby ice on one side of a fracture may override that on the other side to produce hummocked ice. Hummocked ice, and ice in pressure ridges, may attain thicknesses of up to 100 feet or so.

The movement of the pack-ice of the polar seas is influenced by wind, but also, to a greater degree, by currents. Large amounts of Arctic ice are brought into the open Atlantic by the East Greenland current.

Recent studies of the movements of large ice-floes, on which semi-permanent observing stations have been established, reveal that pack-ice originating in the shelf-seas of northern U.S.S.R., drifts into the open North Atlantic between Greenland and Spitsbergen. In contrast, the pack-ice formed on the American side of the polar basin does not readily escape into the open Atlantic. This ice is, in general, thicker—because it is older—than the ice of the eastern Arctic Basin.

Although the Kara, Laptev, East Siberian and Chukchi Seas are icebound for the entire year, navigation is possible, with ice-breaker assistance, for about four months in each year.

In high latitudes in winter the quantity of heat received from the Sun is considerably less than that lost from the sea. If the sea temperature falls to less than about $-2°$ C., sea-ice will form. The temperature at which sea-ice forms is a function of salinity: the higher is the salinity the lower is the freezing temperature.

Freezing of the sea is first indicated by a greasy appearance of the surface after which ice crystals, forming frazil, become visible. Frazil ice continues to grow until the sea is covered with slush, which gradually forms into flat, roughly circular-shaped masses with upturned edges, known as pancake ice. Pancake ice ultimately forms larger ice areas called ice-floes.

Arctic ice, which drifts southwards into the western part of the North Atlantic during spring and summer, presents a serious menace to shipping. Perhaps the greatest ice tragedy of all times was the sinking of the *Titanic* in 1912 with the loss of more than 1500 lives. It was as a result of this disaster that the maritime nations of the world held, in 1913, an international convention for the safety of life at sea. One of the most important suggestions made at the conference led to the establishment of the International Ice Patrol, the management of which is undertaken by the United States Coast Guard Service.

The principal danger to shipping in the fog-bound Grand Banks region of the North Atlantic is the iceberg. Icebergs calved on the East Greenland coast do not present a serious menace to shipping, as they soon melt during their journey southwards into warmer waters. Most of the bergs which present the hazard to shipping in the North Atlantic are calved from tide-water glaciers of West Greenland. Most bergs are calved into Baffin Bay and are carried southwards into the shipping-lanes by the cold Labrador current. After journeying some 1800 miles or so, taking some three seasons to make the journey, many of these bergs disintegrate before reaching the shipping-lanes and many run ashore on the rugged coasts of Labrador and Newfoundland, so that, according to informed reports, no more than about one in 20 bergs calved from West Greenland glaciers reach the Grand Banks region.

The most dangerous months for icebergs in the North Atlantic are May and June.

The sea-ice surrounding the ice continent of Antarctica expands enormously during winter when, to the south of the open Atlantic it extends for about 1000 miles from the shore. The Antarctic sea-ice here is more extensive than elsewhere in the Southern Ocean. Antarctic ice-floes are less restricted in their movements than their Arctic counterparts; and rapid movements, up to about 40 miles per day, are common.

The icebergs of the southern hemisphere are calved not from glaciers but from the so-called shelf ice of Antarctica, this being the seaward extension of the Antarctic ice-cap. The shelf ice terminates at a steep cliff known as the ice barrier. In contrast to the rugged, towering North Atlantic bergs, those of the southern hemisphere are tabular or prismatic in shape. Antarctic bergs may have enormous dimensions compared with those of the North Atlantic, and flat-topped tabular bergs having lengths exceeding 100 miles have been observed.

Glacier bergs are usually greenish in colour compared with the glistening white bergs of the Southern Ocean. Glacier bergs contain large quantities of morainic material and float with smaller free-boards than the bergs of Antarctica which are normally composed of pure ice and snow.

CHAPTER 5

ATLANTIC SEAS

1. Introduction

A sea, according to the oceanographer's definition, is a considerable sheet of oceanic water partly enclosed by land. If we accept this definition, all the particular bays, gulfs and straits, and other inlets we shall mention, are seas. There is no generally-accepted meaning attached to the term sea, and there is certainly not much in common between the water bodies known as the North Sea, Caspian Sea (which is not a sea according to the definition given), Caribbean Sea and Sargasso Sea.

To the Greeks of antiquity, there was only one sea—*The Sea* or *Thalassos*—which is now called the Mediterranean Sea. In contrast to the waters of Thalassos, those of *Okeanus* or *The Ocean*, which was believed to encircle the habitable Earth, were unexplored and unknown until the time when the Mediterranean seamen ventured forth through the Pillars of Hercules to seek trade with the peoples of the Atlantic seaboard of Africa and North-west Europe.

The North Atlantic has been known by seamen since the Golden Age of Discovery initiated by the voyages of the Portuguese Prince Henry's adventurous navigators, as the Western Ocean. The Western Ocean has always been thought of as the ocean of storms and wild seas. The rugged, rock-strewn coast of much of North-west Europe bears witness to the fury of Atlantic storm-waves. The mariners of the North-western European littoral have learnt their seafaring craft in a harsh nursery; and it is little wonder that Norwegians, Danes, Dutch, Germans, French and British, rank among the finest seamen of the world.

The Atlantic Ocean of the oceanographer is normally subdivided by geographers into three parts, named respectively the Arctic, North Atlantic, and South Atlantic Oceans. The Arctic Ocean occupies the Arctic Basin which lies to the north of the line of large islands, notably Iceland, Greenland and Baffin Island, which stretches between the coasts of North-west Europe and North-east Canada. To the south of these islands lies the North Atlantic, which is separated arbitrarily from the South Atlantic by the Equator.

The Arctic Ocean is described by oceanographers as a *mediterranean* sea. This type of sea is a large division of the hydrosphere which, like the classical Mediterranean (which is the type example) is almost landlocked. The waters of the Arctic Ocean are almost hemmed in to the south by the Atlantic islands which lie between Europe and North America, and by the two principal coastlines of northern Canada and northern U.S.S.R., which meet at the shallow and narrow Bering Strait which separates Alaska from Soviet Asia.

The Arctic Ocean, because of its unique physico-oceanographical character, is often considered, even by oceanographers, as a unit separate and distinct from the Atlantic. This does not mean that the waters of the Arctic seas are independent of those of the Atlantic or the Pacific, and it is useful to keep in mind that the world-ocean is physically indivisible. In other words no oceanic water-body is completely independent of other such bodies.

Because of the irregularities in the boundaries between continents and oceans it becomes convenient, and indeed necessary, to sub-divide the major oceanic divisions of the hydrosphere into smaller units such as seas, gulfs, bays and sounds.

2. Arctic Seas

Following in the wake of rapid advances recently made in the scientific exploration and study of the Arctic region, the details of the topography of the Arctic Basin are now being revealed. A significant feature of the Arctic Basin is its exceedingly wide continental shelf.

The Arctic Basin proper is centrally divided by the Lomonosov Ridge, a complex submarine mountain system which extends across the Polar Basin between North Greenland and the continental shelf in the vicinity of the New Siberian Islands. The deep basin on the Canadian side of the Lomonosov Ridge is called the Laurentian Basin, and that on the other side, the Angar Basin. The Angar Basin is separated from the Greenland Basin to the south by a relatively shallow and narrow ridge called the Nansen Rise. The Greenland Basin lies to the north-west of the Jan Mayen Ridge, to the south-east of which is the Norwegian Basin. The Norwegian Basin is hemmed in to the south by a shallow submarine plateau known as the Iceland–Faeroes Rise.

The marginal seas of the Arctic Ocean stand on the wide continental shelf for which reason they are known as shelf-seas. The Barents, Kara, Laptev, East Siberian, and Chukchi Seas, are the principal shelf seas which wash the northern coasts of the Soviet Union.

The Barents Sea is framed by North Norway and the U.S.S.R. on the south; by the Arctic Archipelago of Novaya Zembla on the east; by Franz Joseph Land on the north; and by the islands of the Spitsbergen Archipelago and Bear Island on the west. This ice-encumbered Arctic sea takes its name after the famous Dutch navigator-explorer Willem Barents who voyaged here during the closing decade of the 16th century. It was during an Arctic voyage that Barents met his death in 1597. Nearly three centuries afterwards, in 1871, the hut in which Barents wintered in Novaya Zembla, together with many relics of his ill-fated expedition were discovered. Four years after, part of Barents' journal was found and this, together with several relics, are still preserved in the Netherlands.

An important inlet of the Barents Sea is the White Sea. Archangel, whose famous and commodious harbour stands on the River Dwina, is often referred to as the snow-covered back entrance to the Soviet Union.

The Kara Sea, which lies between the Soviet mainland and Novaya Zembla, extends eastwards to Cape Chelyuskin In the south-west the Kara Sea penetrates deeply into the mainland at Kara Bay. Flowing into the Kara Sea are the great Siberian rivers Ob and Yenesei which drain the vast steppe and forest lands which lie between the Urals and the Central Siberian Plateau The River Ob, with its great tributary the Irtysh, enters the Kara Sea by way of the Gulf of Ob which is some 50 miles wide over a distance of no less than 500 miles The accessibility of the Kara Sea was demonstrated in 1869 and, after Nordenskjöld voyaged through it in 1875, it was considered to be suitable as part of a sea-route between European Russia and Siberia.

East of the Taimyr Peninsula, which terminates at Cape Chelyuskin, the most northerly point of the mainland of the Soviet Union, lies the Laptev Sea which extends eastwards to the New Siberian Islands. The Laptev Sea, which lies to the north of the Yakut Province of Russia, is sometimes called the Nordenskjöld Sea. It is separated from the Kara Sea by the archipelago of Severnaya Zembla, and into it flows the long Siberian River Lena.

Between the New Siberian Islands and Wrangel Island lies the East Siberian Sea; and to the east of Wrangel Island lies the Chukchi Sea which washes the shores of north-east Siberia and Alaska.

The Chukchi Sea is linked to the Bering Sea, the most northerly marginal sea of the great Pacific Ocean, by way of the Bering Strait. The Bering Strait, which is no more than about 50 miles wide, separates the worlds of Russia and the West. It is ice-covered in winter and is believed, by anthropologists, to have provided the migration route for the early Asian folk who first peopled the American continent.

The shelf-seas, which extend from Norway's North Cape to the Bering Strait, have witnessed generations of Arctic explorers intent upon discovering a North-east Passage to China and the Spice Islands of the Far East. The search for the North-east Passage was long and arduous and many renowned navigators perished in their attempts at discovering it.

The Bering Strait was first discovered, by the Danish explorer Captain Vitus Bering, in 1728. Bering was commissioned by Peter the Great of Russia to find out if America and Asia formed one continent. He journeyed by land from Siberia to the Pacific coast of Kamschatka, and later discovered the narrow strait between Asia and America which still bears his name.

It was not until 1879 that passage through the polar seas from the open waters of the Atlantic to the Bering Sea in the Pacific had been accomplished. Credit for having been the first to make the long-sought-after North-east Passage belongs to Nils A. E. Nordenskjöld, the Swedish explorer whose ship the *Vega*, passed into the Pacific southwards through the Bering Strait on July 18th, 1879. The performance was repeated in 1918–21 by the famous explorer Captain Roald Amundsen in his ship the *Maud*. At the present time the North-east Passage is the scene of considerable activity during the short summer season from June to September each year. The Soviet ships engaging in this maritime activity are assisted by modern icebreakers and by an efficient meteorological and ice-reporting service.

Perhaps the greatest of all Arctic explorers was Dr. Fridtjof Nansen, the renowned scientist and Norwegian patriot. As a young man, in 1888, Nansen became famous as the first scientist to cross the Greenland ice-cap. His greatest exploratory feat, however, was his remarkable voyage in the *Fram*, undertaken to test the conjecture that the ice-floes of the North Polar Seas drift across the pole towards the east coast of Greenland. The strongest evidence in support of this idea stemmed from the discovery, in 1884, of some equipment from an ill-fated expedition of polar discovery which had been led by the American explorer George Washington De Long. De Long's ship, the *Jeanette*, sank in 1881 off the Siberian coast, and it appeared that parts of the wreck as well as items of equipment drifted across the polar seas and came ashore some three years later on the east coast of Greenland. Driftwood used by the Greenland Eskimoes provided further evidence when it was argued that this must have originated in northern Russia having been carried to the polar seas by the northward-flowing rivers of Siberia. The theory could be proved, argued Nansen, by taking a ship into the Arctic seas as far east as possible and then purposely allowing her to be gripped in the polar ice. If the postulated current exists, the ship would be carried westwards ultimately to enter the open waters of the North Atlantic Ocean.

Nansen, despite opposition from many renowned scientists of his day, pressed forward with plans to build a vessel suitable in every way for his purpose, so that he could put his theory to the crucial test.

In June, 1893, Nansen sailed from Oslo with Captain Otto Sverdrup in command of the famous *Fram*, a small vessel of 128 feet maximum length and of 36 feet extreme breadth. The *Fram* was constructed on a unique design so that she could withstand the effects of sea-ice. Four days after leaving Oslo the islands of Novaya Zembla, which separate the Barents from the Kara Sea, were sighted. From then on the *Fram* was forced through ice-strewn seas until mid-September when Cape Chelyuskin was rounded. Nansen then decided to head northwards towards the main polar ice-pack. By the end of September his sturdy little ship was well and truly frozen in and the long drift across the polar seas began.

In March, 1895, nearly two years after leaving Oslo, Nansen had reckoned that the drift had brought the *Fram* to within about 6°, or 360 miles, of the Earth's geographical pole. On March 14th he and a companion, Frederick Johansen, set off by sledge with a team of dogs in quest of the pole. Although they were unsuccessful in achieving this aim, Nansen and his companion managed to reach the parallel of latitude of 86° 14' N., and had thus been farther north than any man before them. On April 8th Nansen and Johansen set off southwards, not for the *Fram*, which it would have been nigh impossible to have found, but for Franz Joseph Land. They reached land on August 14th, 1895, five whole months after having left the *Fram*. They wintered in Franz Joseph Land and ultimately arrived back in Norway, to be feted and honoured by the whole of the scientific world, on August 13th, 1896.

After Nansen had left the *Fram* for his bid for the pole, the *Fram* continued to drift westwards, under the command of Captain Sverdrup, and eventually she reached open water after an epic voyage—probably the most remarkable on record—on August 20th, 1896.

The shelf-seas on the American side of the Arctic Ocean include the Beaufort Sea, named after the famous Hydrographer of the Navy, Sir Francis Beaufort. This sea is without islands and it occupies a region at which the continental shelf falls steeply on the poleward side into the deep Beaufort Basin.

To the east of the Beaufort Sea is the remarkable Canadian Archipelago, an extensive area of ice-bound sea studded with islands—many of them very large—and with numerous sounds. The largest island of this great archipelago is Baffin Island, separated from Greenland by Baffin Bay, and named after William Baffin the famous English navigator and Arctic explorer of Elizabethan times.

The waters of Baffin Bay, together with those of Davis Strait to the south, occupy a deep basin known as the Baffin Basin. To the south of Baffin Island is the long Hudson Strait named in honour of Henry Hudson, another prominent Arctic explorer of Elizabethan times. Hudson Strait separates Baffin Island from the mainland of Canada. It leads southwards into Hudson Bay and northwards into Foxe Basin, named after the English navigator Luke Foxe. A narrow strait connects Foxe Basin with the Gulf of Boothia, which takes its name after Felix Booth, an alderman of the City of London who financed a 19th-century expedition of discovery for a North-west Passage to China and the Spice Islands of the Far East.

The North-west Passage, like the North-east Passage, which has already been discussed briefly, was a favourite dream of English merchants during the period between the 16th and 19th centuries. The idea of the possibility of a North-west Passage to the rich spice islands of South-east Asia was first advanced by Robert Thorne as far back as 1527. Thorne, in his book *Seven Ways to Cathay* suggested, amongst others, a route to the Far East across the pole of the world. Many English expeditions sallied forth in attempts to discover a North-west Passage. With these bold attempts are associated the names of some of England's greatest seamen, amongst whom were Martin Frobisher, Captain John Davis the famous navigator, Henry Hudson, William Baffin, Luke Foxe: and, in later times, Sir John Ross, Sir James Clark Ross, Sir William Edward Parry and Sir John Franklin.

Captain James Cook, the most renowned of England's scientific navigators, had rediscovered the Bering Strait during the third of his scientific voyages. Part of the aim of this voyage was to discover a route from the Pacific to the Atlantic Ocean across the polar seas to the north of the American continent. Cook, however, failed to prove the existence of a route from the Pacific to the Atlantic.

Following in the spirit of Cook, John Ross became a notable scientific explorer. Ross was appointed by the British Admiralty to command an expedition, to discover the North-west Passage, in 1818. With John Ross sailed a young midshipman named James

Clark Ross, nephew of John Ross and whose name was also to become famous in the splendid history of polar exploration. Second in command of Ross's expeditionary force of two whaling vessels was William Edward Parry, also to become famous as an Arctic explorer.

Ross's first polar voyage of discovery ended in failure, and following two further polar voyages led by Parry, the Admiralty temporarily withdrew support for the search for a North-west Passage. It was Ross's friend Felix Booth who came to his assistance in financing his second Arctic voyage of discovery. It was during this voyage, which began in 1829, that James Clark Ross, who again sailed under his uncle Captain John Ross, located the position of the North Magnetic Pole which, at the time, was in position latitude 70° N., longitude 96° W., in territory which John Ross named, in honour of his supporter, Boothia Felix Land.

Ross's vessel, the *Victory*, was beset in the Arctic ice and he and his comrades spent two winters in her. During this long period extensive exploration and surveying was undertaken. The *Victory* was abandoned as the third winter set in, and it was not until the spring of 1833, after a hazardous sledge journey and a small-boat voyage, that Ross and his companions were rescued. On his return to England the leader of this expedition, which had survived four winters in Arctic conditions, received a well-merited knighthood.

Sir John Ross's nephew James Clark Ross had served on four Arctic expeditions under Sir William Edward Parry, and a fifth, during which he located the North Magnetic Pole, under his uncle Sir John Ross. James Clark Ross is perhaps best remembered for his leadership of the famous Antarctic expedition in quest of the South Magnetic Pole.

Sir John Franklin was chosen in 1845 to lead an Arctic exploratory expedition with the object of finding a route through the Canadian Archipelago to the Bering Strait. This tragic expedition was the sad circumstance which led to the exploration and charting of a large area of the Arctic Ocean and the Canadian Archipelago, by the numerous search-parties which set out to find Franklin and his comrades and to solve what was regarded as the greatest mystery of the 19th century. It was not until the spring of 1859 that the fate of Franklin's expedition came to light during a search organised by Lady Franklin, the wife of the ill-fated leader. This search expedition, under the leadership of Captain Leopold McClintock in the ship *Fox*, left Aberdeen in July, 1857. It subsequently came to light that Franklin had died on June 11th, 1847, and his expeditionary ships had come within a hair's-breadth of completing the North-

west Passage.   Although honour is usually given to Sir John
Franklin as being the true discoverer of the North-west Passage, his
was a hollow victory.

In the early years of the present century Captain Roald
Amundsen planned an Arctic expedition to re-locate the North
Magnetic Pole and to attempt to accomplish the North-west Passage
by sea.   Amundsen's craft was a small sealer named the *Gjoa*.   The
Gjoa left Christiana in June, 1903, with a total complement of six
men.   The vessel remained for two years in King William Island,
during which time magnetic and other surveys were undertaken and
sledging expeditions to the North Magnetic Pole were made.   In
August, 1905, Amundsen with his party left King William Island
and sailed westwards ultimately to pass through the Bering Strait
on July 11th, 1906.   Amundsen, therefore, is credited with being the
first explorer to have negotiated the North-west Passage successfully.

The extensive stretch of water which lies between Norway and
Greenland is the Greenland Sea which, apart from about a third of
its total area adjacent to the coast of Norway, is ice-bound for the
greater part of the year.   Lying between Iceland and Greenland is
the broad Denmark Strait, which also is ice-bound during the
winter months.

3. *Atlantic Coastlines and Drainage*

The North Atlantic Ocean is characterised by an exceptionally
long coastline relative to its area.   The continent of Europe, which
is often regarded itself as being a peninsula of Asia, is a complex
system of peninsulas which allows the waters of the North Atlantic
to penetrate deeply into the heart of the continent.   Associated with
the deeply-indented coastline of Europe are numerous seas, bays,
gulfs and other inlets.   The densely populated European coastlands
abound in excellent harbours, and ocean trading is of great importance to the coastal states of this part of the world.

The western North Atlantic also has its marginal seas.   The
Gulf of Mexico and the Caribbean Sea together form the Central
American mediterranean sea, hemmed in by the long arcuate string
of islands which form the West Indies.   The Central American Sea,
the classical Mediterranean and the Arctic Ocean, are the three
mediterranean-type seas of the Atlantic Ocean.

Although the eastern seaboard of North America is relatively
simple in form, it is not without wide inlets, bays and estuaries,
including the Gulf of St. Lawrence, Long Island Sound, and Delaware
and Chesapeake Bays.

Numerous rivers flow into the North Atlantic Ocean. Almost the whole of the drainage of the continent of Europe terminates in the peripheral seas of the North Atlantic. The rivers Rhine, Elbe, Loire, Seine and Rhône, are important European rivers which empty themselves into the marginal seas of the North Atlantic. It is interesting to note, however, that Europe's longest river, the Volga, drains into an inland terminal drainage basin called the Caspian Sea.

The greater part of African drainage falls into the North Atlantic. The Nile and the Niger which drain the greater part of North Africa are among the longest rivers of the globe. Other African rivers which drain into the North Atlantic are the Volta and the Senegal.

It is perhaps surprising to realise that almost the whole of both North and South America drain into the North Atlantic Ocean. The St. Lawrence, Hudson, and Mississippi Rivers are among the great rivers of North America which drain into this ocean. The waters of the vast Magdalena and those of the even vaster Amazon of South America also drain into the North Atlantic. The greater part of the drainage of Uruguay, Paraguay and Argentina enters the South Atlantic Ocean by way of the River Plate estuary.

4. The Marginal Seas of the Eastern Atlantic

The continental shelf of North-west Europe breaks up the sea area into numerous seas and gulfs. The most extensive shelf-sea of the eastern part of the North Atlantic Ocean is the North Sea. The cold, gray and seldom friendly, waters of the North Sea lie to the east of the British Isles. These are the waters, which wash the shores of many of the maritime States of Europe, in which the seamen of Europe have learnt their art.

The Danish peninsula, which juts northwards into the triangular area formed between southern Norway and Sweden, separates the North Sea from the Baltic Sea. The Baltic is approached through the Skaggerak between Denmark and Norway, and through the Kattegat between Denmark and Sweden, thence through the narrow Sound commanded by the important mediaeval market centre, Copenhagen.

The Baltic Sea leads into the Gulf of Bothnia, which is guarded by the Aaland Islands; the Gulf of Finland at the head of which lies Peter the Great's window on the world, now called Leningrad; and the Gulf of Riga, guarded by the Osel Islands.

The great volume of land drainage which falls into the Baltic Sea and its branches makes it the least saline of all seas. Shut off from the warming influence of the North Atlantic drift current, navigation in the Baltic Sea and its arms, especially in the Gulf of Bothnia, is severely restricted by ice during the winter months.

A remarkable inlet of the North Sea is the Zuider Zee of the Netherlands. The Zuider Zee has in recent times been the scene of land reclamation on a scale which no nation other than the Dutch could even have tackled.

The Strait of Dover links the North Sea with the English Channel, or La Manche of the French. This treacherous stretch of sea lies at the meeting-point of tidal streams from north and west. Its navigable channels are narrow and dangerous and they are seriously hampered by shifting sands. Added to these hazards are winter gales and frequent fog. The density of shipping here is greater than it is anywhere else in the world, as many as 300,000 ship-passages being made through the Strait in a year.

Lying between Ireland and the main island of the United Kingdom is the Irish Sea, which is approached in the north through the narrow North Channel between Scotland and Northern Ireland, and through the broad St. George's Channel in the south between Eire and the Pembroke Peninsula of Wales.

To the south of the Brittany Peninsula lies the Bay of Biscay, with the French and Spanish coasts to east and south respectively. The Bay takes its name from the northern Spanish province of Viscaya. This is a sea which from earliest times has inspired seamen with some degree of awe. The wide-mouthed bay is open to Atlantic gales and its waters are seldom free from swell or waves.

Stretching eastwards from the narrow Strait of Gibraltar, for a distance of more than 2000 miles, are the waters of the Mediterranean.

The relatively simple form of the African Atlantic coastline makes it unnecessary to subdivide the ocean in this locality. Mention must be made, however, of the large embayment which extends from Cape Palmas in Liberia to Cape Lopez in the Congo, and which is bounded by the coastlands of equatorial West Africa, known as the Gulf of Guinea. Into this wide gulf falls the rivers Volta, Niger and Cameroon.

5. Western Atlantic Seas

In the north-western Atlantic the extensive Gulf of St. Lawrence is hemmed in by the western coast of the island of Newfoundland. The narrow channel between the Labrador coast and the northern extremity of Newfoundland is the well-known Belle Isle Strait. The shorter route from North-west Europe to the St. Lawrence is by way of the Belle Isle Strait which, unfortunately, is ice-bound in wintertime. Following the seasonal opening up of the St. Lawrence estuary in springtime, the first ships bound for the St. Lawrence ports of Quebec and Montreal and others, make for Cape Race and thence Cape Ray respectively, at the eastern and western corners of Newfoundland's southern shores, after which they follow the route through the Cabot Strait which separates Newfoundland from Cape Breton Island in Canada's Nova Scotia.

The west coast of the southern lobe of Nova Scotia hems in the Bay of Fundy, noted for its famed fishing fleets and abnormally great tidal ranges of as much as 50 feet or more.

The Central American mediterranean sea comprises two major seas. These are the Gulf of Mexico and the Caribbean Sea which are linked by the Yucatan Channel between the western part of Cuba and the Yucatan Peninsula of Mexico.

The principal topographical features of the Central American mediterranean sea are its five main basins. The waters of the Gulf of Mexico occupy the Mexico Basin. The Yucatan Basin and the deep Cayman Trough, which occupies the area south of Cuba, extends into the Gulf of Yucatan. The Colombia and Venezuela Basins occupy respectively the south-western and south-eastern parts of the Caribbean area.

The greatest known depth, of 7200 metres, within the Centra. American mediterranean, is located in the Cayman Trough at the Bartlett Deep. The greatest known depth in the Atlantic Ocean is 8750 metres. This is found in the Puerto Rico Trench which lies to the north of the passage between Puerto Rico and Hispaniola to the west.

The complex topography of the Central American region as a whole, together with associated seismological and volcanic activity and pronounced gravity anomalies, makes the area one of particular interest to geophysicists.

The Atlantic coastline of Central America from Mexico to eastern Venezuela is deeply indented with many wide gulfs or bays. The Gulf of Campeche lies to the west, and the Gulf of Honduras lies to the east of the Yucatan Peninsula.

The Gulf of Darien washes the shores of Panama and Colombia. The former territory occupies the narrow isthmus through which the Panama Canal has been cut, and which separates the Atlantic from the Pacific Ocean.

To the south of the Gulf of Maracaibo, to which it is linked by a narrow channel, is the remarkable Lake Maracaibo, a shallow fresh-water lake, on the shores and through the bed of which numerous oil-wells have been bored. Through these flow much of the valuable petroleum which brings wealth to Venezuela.

The coastlands of Central America, stretching eastwards from the Isthmus of Panama to the mouths of the Orinoco, formed the Spanish Main. These coastlands, together with the islands of the Caribbean Sea, witnessed the struggle between England and Spain for the supremacy of the High Seas during Elizabethan times. With this romantic region are associated the pirates and buccaneers who have left a corpus of legends behind them thereby supplying numerous novelists and other story-writers with ample material for their needs.

The Caribbean Sea takes its name from the Caribs, the warlike American Indians who occupied the islands of the Lesser Antilles and the adjacent mainland of South America. The Caribs were the folk encountered by Columbus when these islands were first visited by Europeans. At the time of the Great Discoveries the Caribs had not long been in possession of the Lesser Antillean islands, having subdued and eliminated the earlier Arawakan inhabitants. But even this fierce race of men was to succumb to the militant and well-organised Spanish invaders.

The Caribbean Sea extends westwards from the Leeward and Windward Islands for about 1500 miles to the narrow Yucatan Channel which connects it with the Gulf of Mexico. Its average north-south extent is about 500 miles, so that its area is about 75,000 square miles.

Following the European discovery of the New World the Caribbean Sea soon became the scene of one of the greatest territorial scrambles in history. This colourful region, with its turbulent history, has witnessed piracy and plunder on the greatest of scales. The islands and the mainland of the South American continent which form its border still bear the stamp of Spanish, Portuguese, British, French and Dutch. In more recent times the influence of the powerful United States, which lies immediately to the north, has been felt by the whole region.

The narrow Isthmus of Panama, which forms part of the south-west border of the Caribbean Sea, separates the Atlantic from the Pacific by a mere 50 miles or so. This region figured in the 16th and 17th centuries as the important centre used by the Spaniards for transhipping the treasures of the Spanish colonies of the Pacific area to the ships of their Atlantic fleets. It was the ships of these fleets which became the objects of attack by pirates and buccaneers of old.

The Caribbean Sea has, for many centuries, been an important shipping area, but since the opening of the Panama Canal in 1920, it has become a major maritime highway of international importance.

F

To the south of the shoulder of Brazil at about latitude 5° S., the Atlantic coast of the South American continent is relatively simple in outline for nearly 1000 miles. The first major indentation appears in latitude 35° S., at the mouth of the River Plate, on which stand the capital cities Montevideo and Buenos Aires of Uruguay and Argentina respectively.

Between the Plate Estuary and the Magellan Strait, which separates the island of Tierra del Fuego from the mainland of South America, there are three large bays, known respectively as Bahia Blanca, the Gulf of St. Matthew, and the Gulf of St. George.

6. Atlantic Seas of Antarctica

The Drake Passage, between Cape Horn and the Grahamland Peninsula of Antarctica, is the region of westerly gales and the fierce Cape Horn current which made the westbound rounding of Cape Horn the terrible task it was for the sailing-ship captains in the days of sail.

Lying between the Grahamland Peninsula to the west and Coats Land to the east is the deep indentation of the isolated continent of Antarctica known as the Weddell Sea. This Antarctic shelf sea takes its name from Captain James Weddell who, in 1823, reached the highest southerly latitude ever attained up to that time in the sea which now bears his name. The famous London whaling firm of Enderby encouraged their ship captains to explore the waters in which their southern whaling ships operated whenever they had the opportunity, and it was during a whaling voyage that Captain Weddell penetrated as far south as latitude 74° 15'. Another famous Enderby captain was John Biscoe, whose name is given to the sea lying to the east of the Weddell Sea.

PART I

CHAPTER 6

ATLANTIC ISLANDS

1. Introduction

The several divisions of the Earth's water cover, such as seas, gulfs and other oceanic bodies, are all interconnected, so that the world-ocean is a continuum or undivided feature of the planet Earth. The land surfaces, in contrast, are divided or fragmented into parts the dimensions of which vary from those of the great continental land-masses of Eurasia, America, Africa and Australia, to those of the smallest rocks which just protrude above the sea surface at tidal Low Water. All of these land fragments are islands in the sense that they are surrounded by sea. The term island, however, is usually reserved for the smaller land-masses excluding barren rocks and shoals which dry at Low Water.

Islands are usually classified as continental and oceanic or pelagic. Continental islands are those which stand upon continental shelves, such as the British Isles, or those which are continental fragments, such as Greenland which, in geological times past, were joined to other such fragments. Oceanic islands, on the other hand, include only those which rise above the sea from the deep ocean bed.

Continental shelf islands may originate from any of several causes. Submergence of coastal regions may give rise to islands which form from the higher parts of such regions following the the inundation of the lower parts. On the other hand shelf islands may be formed by a general rise in sea-level following the melting of ice after a glacial maximum. Sea-level may rise, or submergence of the land take place, so that ultimately the sea may break across an isthmus, so initiating the formation of an island from land which hitherto had been a peninsula. Rising of sea-level or submergence of a coastland may give rise to the formation of a group of islands between which are shallow inlets or navigable channels or sounds. Such a group of islands is an archipelago, a general name taken from the island-studded Grecian Archipelago of the Eastern Mediterranean.

A continental island may be formed as a consequence of faulting or folding of crustal rocks—a fault zone often being occupied by a deep channel between two adjacent islands which formerly were

73

joined together. Again, a continental island may be formed by action of the sea which, by erosion of relatively weak cliff-rock due to waves and tidal action, may cause a continental fragment to be detached from the parent continent. Examples exist of Atlantic continental islands formed by all the ways mentioned above.

Continental islands have geological structures and rock formations which are characteristic of those found in the adjacent continent. The architecture of oceanic islands, however, is related to the ocean bed in their vicinity. The projection above sea-level of the ocean floor, through volcanic action or earth movements, results in the formation of an oceanic island. The Earth's crustal rocks, which floor the ocean basins, are basaltic in character. The truly oceanic islands are, therefore, invariably composed of the igneous rock basalt, for which reason they are often known as basaltic islands.

The curious island-arcs exemplified in the Atlantic by those of the Antillean Islands of the West Indies, and the Southern Antilles in Antarctica, owe their origin to a combination of large-scale earth movements and volcanic activity.

2. Greenland, Iceland and the Faeroes

The largest Atlantic island is Greenland which, apart from island-continents, is the world's largest island. It lies almost wholly within the Arctic Circle and seven-eighths of its area of about 800,000 square miles is ice-covered. The meridianal length of Greenland is about 1600 miles and the island stretches northwards from Cape Farewell, which is on a small island off the southern tip of Greenland in latitude 60° N., to the 87th parallel of latitude. Greenland, together with Iceland, the Faeroes and Shetlands, stand on a sub-oceanic ridge which has an important effect on the deep circulation of the Atlantic and Arctic waters.

Norsemen settled in Greenland as early as the ninth century, its discovery having been made by Eric the Red in A.D. 876. It was rediscovered by European explorers during the Age of Discovery in the 16th century. Greenland now falls under the sovereignty of Denmark, a control established in 1729. Of its 25,000 inhabitants most are Eskimoes; the remainder, numbering no more than about 1000, being Danish.

Greenland supports an ice-cap formed by an immense lens of ice the thickness of which in its central part is said to be about 10,000 feet. The first crossing of the Greenland ice-cap was made by the famous Norwegian explorer and scientist Fridtjof Nansen and five companions in 1888. Nansen reached an altitude of 8900 feet in latitude $64\frac{1}{2}°$ N.

The Greenland ice-cap is a region of perpetually high atmospheric pressure, the outblowing cold winds from which having a marked influence on the climate of the North Atlantic.

The coasts of Greenland are deeply indented and glaciers debouch into the sea along fjords bounded by high, rocky mountains called by the Eskimo name *nunataks*.

Greenland is well known for being the only commercial natural source of the mineral cryolite which is used as a catalyst in the electrolytic production of aluminium.

The large island of Iceland, which is separated from Greenland by the Denmark Strait, lies at the northern extremity of the Mid-Atlantic Ridge. Its northern coastland lies just within the Arctic Circle.

Iceland consists of a table-land built up of basaltic rocks. The inhabited parts of the island are confined to coastal areas, the table-land being occupied by snow-fields and barren lava flows. Mount Hekla, the most famous of Iceland's numerous volcanoes, was last in eruption in 1845. In historic times some 25 Icelandic volcanoes are known to have erupted. Frequently there are outbursts of submarine volcanic activity off the south-west peninsula of Reykjanes in which steaming volcanic islands come into being later to be eroded by the action of Atlantic waves.

The first submarine eruption witnessed off Iceland occurred in 1783. The reason for the frequent volcanic eruptions that take place in Iceland is that the island stands on the Mid-Atlantic Ridge. The geological and geophysical evidence, as we have discussed in Chapter 2, suggests that Iceland is being stretched in an east-west direction and that the present area of volcanic activity, which covers about one-third of the country, lies along the zone of greatest stretching. It is interesting to reflect that of the total volcanic material extruded since A.D., 1500 no less than one-third has been produced in Iceland.

In recent historical times volcanic eruptions on the Mid-Atlantic Ridge have been frequent. In 1961 a major eruption took place in Askja in Iceland, and in the same year the volcanic eruption in Tristan da Cunha forced the island's population to leave. In 1963, a submarine eruption resulted in the formation of the island of Surtsey. This remarkable island, named after the giant *Surtur* who, in Norse mythology, is associated with fire, was first sighted at a distance of no more than about half a mile, from an Icelandic fishing-vessel in the early hours of the morning of November 14th,

1963. The depth of the sea in the locality before the eruption was about 70 fathoms, and on the second day of the eruption the island's highest point was about 30 feet above sea-level. In five days Surtsey grew to about 200 feet in height and about 2000 feet in length.

Associated with volcanic activity in Iceland are numerous geysers and hot springs, and boiling lakes and sulphur springs.

The climate of Iceland is tempered by the warming influence of the North Atlantic drift current. During winter the Arctic ice encroaches southwards and reaches Iceland's north coast. This, coupled with cold polar sea-currents which sometimes reach the island, is responsible for the chilly weather in wintertime. Seals and whales, and numerous species of sea-birds, abound in the waters surrounding Iceland. Fish, especially cod, are abundant in Icelandic waters, and the fisheries of Iceland provide the country's principal source of revenue.

To the east of Iceland lie the Danish Faero Islands. These, the so-called Sheep Islands, are situated midway between Iceland and the Shetlands. Of the 21 islands in the archipelago 17 are inhabited. These islands have a basaltic foundation and are capped in places with sedimentaries amongst which brown coal is found. The treeless islands are high and rugged and the coasts are fjorded in places. Although sheep are numerous other domesticated animals are few. Cod fishing in the surrounding waters is important and so also is whaling.

3. The Canadian Archipelago

To the west of Greenland are the Canadian Arctic Islands. The largest of these is Baffin Island which lies to the west of the wide Baffin Bay. At the extreme north, Greenland is separated from Ellesmere Island in the Canadian Archipelago by a very narrow strait. To the west of Ellesmere Island are the Sverdrup and Parry Islands to the south of which are the large Victoria and Banks Islands. Permanent ice is to be found in Ellesmere and Baffin Islands; but the islands in the western part of the archipelago are too low-lying, and experience too little precipitation for permanent ice to form. The channels between the western islands of the archipelago are shallow and ice-encumbered, factors which made the early attempts at discovering the North-west Passage difficult, and which still hamper sea communications in the Canadian Arctic region. To the west of the Canadian Arctic islands lies the broad expanse of the Beaufort Sea in which islands are absent.

The question of jurisdiction over the Arctic islands to the north of Canada came to a head with the discovery of important oil-fields in Alaska. The Americans and the Canadians see great economic possibilities in the Arctic regions, and the latter are making it clear that American investment and the presence of American technicians in the north, in no way derogates from Canadian sovereignty. Canada is aware of the possibility of losing Arctic islands, which she claims are hers, unless her claims are demonstrated by occupation; and many Canadians would like to see Canadian troops stationed in the far north, as a means of establishing the Canadian presence.

4. *Arctic Islands of Europe and Asia*

Some 500 miles to the north of Norway's North Cape lies the Arctic archipelago generally called Spitsbergen, but by the Norwegians, under whose political control the islands fall, it is known as Svalbard. Spitsbergen, so named because of its abundance of sharp-pointed lofty mountain peaks, lies midway between Greenland and the Soviet archipelago of Novaya Zembla.

The Norwegians formally took possession of Spitsbergen in 1925 since when valuable coal deposits have led to a seasonal population in summer, mainly of mine-workers, who number some 4000 or 5000. Many of the islands are glaciated although glaciers do not calve icebergs of any considerable size.

The Spitsbergen Archipelago consists of continental islands in which the most ancient sedimentary rocks occur. Coal is to be found in considerable quantities, and during the brief summer season, when the coastal waters are ice-free, coal is shipped for Norway and other European countries.

Midway between Spitsbergen and the North Cape is the small Bear Island, the shallow waters around which abound in fish and which are worked extensively by British and other European deep-sea trawlermen.

To the east of Spitsbergen, and straddling the 80th parallel of latitude, is the Arctic archipelago known as Franz Joseph Land, the most northerly land in the eastern hemisphere. Franz Joseph Land comes under the sovereignty of the Soviet Union.

It was on one of the islands of the Franz Joseph group that, in 1894, Alfred Harmsworth (later to become Lord Northcliffe) financed the setting up of a permanent base from which a journey might be made to the North Pole some 500 miles to the north. The initial expedition was led by F. G. Jackson. As a result of Nansen's discovery of a deep ocean basin to the north of Franz Joseph Land, the attempt to reach the Pole from the base in Franz Joseph Land was abandoned. It was on June 17th, 1896, that Nansen, returning from his bid to reach the Pole by journey across the polar ice after leaving the *Fram*, held his dramatic meeting with Jackson on Franz Joseph Land. It was Jackson's expeditionary ship the *Windward* which brought Nansen and his companion back to civilisation after their memorable voyage in the Arctic seas between 1893 and 1896.

The line joining Spitsbergen and Franz Joseph Land forms the northern boundary of the Barents Sea. The eastern boundary of this sea is formed by the Arctic islands of Novaya Zembla.

Novaya Zembla, which is part of the U.S.S.R., consists of two large islands separated by a narrow 56-mile-long strait. The two islands together form an elongated crescent or scimitar-shaped structure some 600 miles long. To the south of Novaya Zembla is Vaygach Island. These islands form a northern extension of a branch of the Ural Mountain system, the traditional boundary zone between Europe and Asia.

Lying to the north of Cape Chelyuskin on the Taimyr Peninsula is the group of Soviet islands known as Severnaya Zembla. These mark the western boundary of the Laptev Sea.

The eastern boundary of the Laptev Sea is marked by the New Siberian Islands and the Lyakhov Islands, the former being the more northerly of the two groups. The Lyakhov Islands are separated from the Soviet mainland by the Laptev Strait. They take their name from a Russian merchant who visited them and first described them in 1770.

Lying between the East Siberian Sea and the Chukchi Sea is Wrangel Island, named after a German explorer who investigated in 1824, but failed to discover, the island which was reported by Chukchi natives living in the East Siberian coastlands. The name was given to it in 1867 by an American explorer. The Russians first landed on Wrangel Island in 1911. A Canadian attempt to claim the island was frustrated by Soviet Russia whose claim is not now disputed.

5. *Shelf Islands of Europe*

The continental shelf of North-west Europe includes the British Isles and the Danish Archipelago, as well as numerous islands in the Baltic Sea and its arms.

Continental islands are of interest to zoologists and botanists as well as to geologists, and often these scientists are able mutually to assist each other in their investigations. The careful study of the plant-life and animal-life of an island and that of the adjacent continent, for instance, often provides clues which assist the geologist in estimating the period when the island was first separated from the mainland. The separation of an island from the mainland generally leads to an absence on the island of species of flora and fauna more recent in origin than that of the time of separation.

The observation that certain land animals are common to the British Isles and the European continent provides evidence that the British Isles were at one time physically united with Europe. Moreover, the evidence that the flora and fauna of Ireland is poorer than that of the adjacent continent is proof that the Strait of Dover was formed after the formation of the Irish Sea.

To a Frenchman or Dutchman the British Isles may be regarded as being no more than a group of small islands lying off their respective coasts. Yet the peoples of this group of small islands have played a major part, if not the predominant role, in the world's history during the last three centuries. In this respect the islands of Britain may be said to have occupied the very centre of the world during this long period. The narrow Dover Strait has served to isolate Britain physically from the European continent; yet, by way of England's so-called 'continental pivot', at which the two major linguistic frontiers of Western Europe meet, the British have profited immensely from the influence of the Latin and Teutonic peoples of the continent.

The historical geology, or stratigraphy, of the British Isles is probably more complex than that of any comparable area in the whole world. Of the strata which outcrop in Britain every geological system, and almost every geological period, is represented. A great diversity of rock types, including those of igneous as well as sedimentary origin, has given rise to a wealth of mineral resources which served the British well during their rise to political and economic power.

6. The North-east Atlantic Islands

Guarding the Gulf of St. Lawrence, giving access to this large water-body by way of the Belle Isle Strait to its north and the wider Cabot Strait to the south, is the large and rugged island of Newfoundland. Geologically Newfoundland is the northern extension of the Appalachian mountain system of eastern North America. Fish and forest products are the principal items of commerce in Newfoundland's economy, although the mining of iron-ore and other minerals, including copper and zinc, is an activity of growing importance.

To the south-east of Newfoundland are the well-known Grand Banks of Newfoundland. These form a huge submarine plateau some 420 miles by 350 miles at the meeting-place of warm and cold ocean currents which bring about the fog for which the area is notorious.   The waters overlying the Grand Banks, and other banks to the south-west lying off the coast of Nova Scotia, abound in fish. These waters are fished extensively by European as well as by American fishermen.

To the west of Newfoundland, within the Gulf of St. Lawrence, is the island of Anticosti with an area exceeding 3000 square miles, densely forested with valuable timber resources.

One of the Canadian Maritime Provinces, lying in the Gulf of St. Lawrence, is the low-lying Prince Edward Island.   This, the smallest province of Canada, was named in 1798 after the English Duke of Kent.

South-east of Nova Scotia lies the dreaded and dangerous Sable Island, a shrinking sandy island some 20 miles long and a mile, wide, and the scene of numerous shipwrecks.

Lying to the east of the mouth of the Hudson River is Long Island which stretches for almost 120 miles in a direction parallel to the Connecticut coast from which it is separated by Long Island Sound.   This island is an overspill region for the city of New York, a rich market gardening area, and a playground for the people of the great American metropolis.

From the south of the mouth of the Chesapeake to Key West in Florida the coast is one of emergence.   Characteristic of an emerging coast is the existence of numerous off-lying spits and bars and low-lying sandy islands on the landward side of which are shallow lagoons and sounds.   This type of coast is known technically as a *haff-nehrung* coast, the type example of which is the Baltic coast of Germany.   Perhaps the most splendid example of this type of coast exists in the Gulf of Mexico to the west of the Mississippi delta where the long sand-spits, or nehrungen, extend unbroken in some instances for hundreds of miles.

7. *Central American Islands*

The Central American Sea, comprising the Gulf of Mexico and the Caribbean Sea, is separated from the open Atlantic by the islands of the West Indies which collectively form a huge natural breakwater which breasts the open Atlantic to the east.

The West Indian Archipelago is sometimes called the Antilles. It stretches in arcuate form from Florida and Yucatan to Venezuela. The West Indian islands are of great diversity in respect of geological structure, size and other physical characteristics.   They are grouped into the Bahamas; the Greater Antilles, which include the large islands of Cuba, Jamaica, Hispaniola and Puerto Rico; and the

Lesser Antilles, which include some dozens of islands stretching from the Virgins to Trinidad. The Lesser Antilles are divided into the Windward and the Leeward Islands.

The name West Indies stems from Columbus' mistaken idea that the islands he had discovered by sailing westwards from Europe were those of the fabulous Indies or Spice Islands. The name Antilles is derived from Antilia or Anthelia—a region away from the sunrise—the name given by Mediaeval geographers to the imaginary land which filled the unknown west.

The islands of the West Indies are the emergent parts of sub-marine-mountain systems which are continued in the northern part of South America and in Central America.

The Bahamas form an archipelago comprising some 30 islands and about 3000 or so islets and rocks. It extends for about 750 miles from the Florida Strait to Turks Island off the north coast of Hispaniola. The islands are low-lying and are of coral formation. Columbus' first landfall in the New World was one of the islands of the Bahamas which he named San Salvador, but which is now called Watling Island.

The Bahamas were depopulated by the early Spanish settlers in the West Indies who forced the natives to work in the mines and sugar mills of Hispaniola. English settlement began in the 17th century. The motto on the arms of the Bahamas is 'Expulsis Piratis Restituta Commercia', by which we are reminded that the islands and the cays of the Bahamas were favourite haunts of pirates in times gone by.

Cuba, the sugar mill and the cigar factory of the Antilles, is the largest island of the West Indies. Formerly a Spanish possession, it is now an independent State under the control of a Communist dictator. Cuba is separated from the peninsula of Florida by the Florida Strait, and from the peninsula of Yucatan by the Yucatan Channel. To the south of Cuba lies the beautiful jewel of the Caribbean, Jamaica.

Jamaica occupies a strategic position in the Caribbean, lying as it does on the direct route from the busy Windward Passage between Cuba and Hispaniola, to the Panama Canal. She is the producer of large quantities of sugar, bananas, coffee, and a wide variety of spices, including pimento or all-spice and ginger. Much of Jamaica's revenue stems from her valuable tourist attractions which include exquisite mountain and coastal scenery; a pleasant climate; and colourful and gay, albeit poor, Jamaican people themselves.

To the east of Cuba, across the Windward Passage, is the large island of Hispaniola which is divided politically between the negro republic of Haiti, and the Dominican Republic to the east. Less black than Haiti and less white than Cuba, the Dominican Republic is often referred to as the Mulatto Republic.

The island of Puerto Rico, the smallest of the islands of the Greater Antilles, became a possession of the United States after the Spanish-American War of 1898.

To the north of Puerto Rico is the deep Puerto Rico Trench in which the greatest Atlantic depths are to be found. Puerto Rico's most important crop is sugar but tobacco and coffee, as well as tropical fruits, such as orange, pineapple and grapefruit, are also grown in abundance.

About two-thirds of Puerto Ricans are of Spanish descent. For three centuries this rich island was the penal settlement for Spanish criminals. Those condemned to death were given the alternative choice of serving on the sugar plantations virtually as slaves.

The density of population in Puerto Rico exceeds that of most of the West Indian islands, and the migration of large numbers of Puerto Ricans to the United States has relieved the population pressure on the island but created social problems in the city of New York with its ever-increasing Puerto Rican minority group.

To the east of Puerto Rico lies an outer chain of islands including the Virgin Islands, Anguilla, St. Bartholomew, Antigua, Eastern Guadeloupe, Barbadoes, Tobago and Trinidad. Within the arc formed by these, lies an inner chain of islands including Saba, St. Lucia, St. Vincent, the Grenadines and Grenada. This arcuate line of islands is continued westwards through the islands which fringe the northern coast of Venezuela from Margarita to Bonaire, Curaçao and Aruba. On the Atlantic side of this double chain of islands a line of coralline structures exists. Among these are the Florida Peninsula, the Bahamas, Anguilla, Barbuda, eastern Barbados, and southern Trinidad. All the islands of the West Indies, apart from these coralline structures, are mountainous with rugged surfaces. The mountains of the West Indies are highest in Haiti where they attain heights exceeding 10,000 feet.

The Leeward Islands form the more northerly group of the Lesser Antilles. The Virgin Islands lie to the east of Puerto Rico. Most of the islands of this group are British, although St. Thomas, St. Croix, and St. John, come under United States' sovereignty, having been purchased from Denmark in 1917. The small island of Sombrero, lying to the east of the Virgins, gives its name to the wide passage, commonly used by oil tankers trading between Europe and the Dutch islands of Curaçao and Aruba and the oil-ports of Venezuela.

To the east of the Virgin Islands is the coralline island of Anguilla, with its important salt ponds. To the south of Anguilla is St. Martin, partly French and partly Dutch and, like Anguilla, an important salt producer. The volcanic islands of St. Eustatius and Saba are Dutch islands in the Leeward group. The beautiful volcanic island of Saba rises abruptly from the sea-bed. The principal settlement, appropriately named Bottom, stands on the crater floor access to which is gained by The Ladder, a long rock staircase leading upwards from the island's single landing-place.

St. Kitts, often called the Mother Colony of the West Indies, being the first island on which an English settlement was made, is also a volcanic island. Antigua, the seat of government of the British Leeward Islands, lies about 40 miles to the east of Nevis, the historic island with which Lord Nelson is associated. Montserrat, a peculiarity of which is the decided Irish brogue spoken by its inhabitants, is famous for its limes.

The twin islands of Guadeloupe formed France's largest West Indian colony, and it is now a French Overseas Department. The highest peak here, La Soufrière, which rises to 4900 feet, is an active volcano. The island of Martinique is also a French Overseas Department. This island lies between the British islands of Dominica and St. Lucia to its north and south respectively. Martinique is of historic interest in that it is the birthplace of Napoleon's wife, the Empress Josephine. It is a very rugged volcanic island, the highest elevation being Mont Pelée, the Bald Mountain, the eruption of which in 1902 completely destroyed the town of St. Pierre which, at that time, was the principal commercial centre of the island.

Dominica is the largest of the British Leeward Islands. It takes its name from its having been discovered by Columbus on Sunday, November 3rd, 1493. It is well known for its volcanic activity and for its boiling lake.

St. Lucia, whose motto is 'A Safe Anchorage', has a deeply-indented coast. In the days of coal-burning ships it was an important bunkering station. This island, together with St. Vincent, the Grenadines and Grenada, belongs to the Windward Islands. St. Vincent is noted for its arrowroot and Grenada for its nutmegs. The Grenadines are the several small islands located between St. Vincent and Grenada.

To the east of the Windward Islands lies Barbados, named by the Portuguese on account of the bearded fig-trees they found there. From 1605 Barbados has been a British possession. It is the most easterly of the West Indian islands, and for this reason great strategic and commercial importance was attached to it in times gone by. Barbados is a low-lying island almost encircled by coral reefs. It is an important producer of sugar and cotton. Barbados is sometimes called the Flying Fish Island, on account of the large numbers of flying fish which are caught in the waters surrounding it.

To the south of the Windward Islands lie Trinidad and Tobago. Tobago, a ward of Trinidad, is famous as the island from which Daniel Defoe drew his descriptions for his immortal *Robinson Crusoe*.

The island of Trinidad is geologically a part of the South American continent. It is separated from the mainland by the Gulf of Paria, into which many of the mouths of the River Orinoco fall. Trinidad is an important producer of petroleum, and is famous for its pitch lake, from which Trinidad asphalt is obtained.

Lying off the South American mainland to the east of the Gulf of Maracaibo are the Dutch A, B, C islands of Aruba, Bonaire and Curaçao. Curaçao is the largest of the Dutch West Indian islands and its colourful capital Willemstad is noted for its picturesque Dutch-style buildings. Important petroleum refineries are established on the islands of Aruba and Curaçao where large quantities of Venezuelan crude oil, from the nearby oil-fields of Lake Maracaibo, as well as from the eastern oil-fields of Venezuela, are refined.

8. South-west Atlantic Islands

The only continental islands of note in the western Atlantic south of Trinidad are the Falkland Islands and Tierra del Fuego.

The Falklands form an archipelago lying about 250 miles off the mainland of South America. The two principal members of the group are East and West Falkland which are separated by the Falkland Sound. In addition to these two large islands the archipelago consists of some 200 small islands clustered within an area of about 7000 square miles. The coastlines of the large islands are deeply-indented and good harbours are plentiful.

The Falkland Islands were discovered by the English navigator John Davis in 1592, and they take their name from Lord Falkland who was killed at the Battle of Newbury in 1690. The islands are linked geologically with Patagonia with which they are connected by a submarine plateau.

At the southern extremity of the continent of South America lies the archipelago of Tierra del Fuego, which is separated from the mainland by the Magellan Strait. The archipelago is divided politically between Argentina and Chile. The name 'Land of Fire' was given to it by Magellan on account of the numerous native settlements, each illuminated at night by its camp-fire. Sheep-farming on the main island is particularly profitable.

About 1000 miles to the east of the South American mainland, and lying roughly in the same latitude as the Falkland Islands, is the island of South Georgia, a dependency of the Falklands. Captain James Cook claimed the island for Great Britain in 1775. The sole industries of South Georgia are whaling and whale processing.

Captain Cook also claimed for Great Britain the islands of the South Shetland group which, with Grahamland of Antarctica, are dependencies of the Falklands. The northernmost island of the South Shetlands is about 500 miles south of the Falklands. Volcanic activity is considerable in this region.

To the east of the South Shetlands are the South Orkneys, and to the east of this archipelago is the island-arc formed by the South Sandwich chain. These islands, as well as the South Orkneys, are dependencies of the Falkland Islands.

To the east of the South Sandwich Islands lies the deep oceanic trough known as the South Sandwich Trench, in which great oceanic depths have been sounded.

9. The Ridge Islands of the Atlantic

The nearest oceanic islands which stand on the Mid-Atlantic Ridge southwards of Iceland are those of the Azores group. The Azores Archipelago belongs to Portugal. The volcanic islands of the Azores rise steeply from the ocean bed, the highest elevation being attained on the island of Pico at 7613 feet above sea-level.

The Azores, lying as they do to the west of the Iberian Peninsula, was the rendezvous of the treasure-ships bound homewards to Spain from the West Indies during Elizabethan times when Britain was at enmity with Spain. Here, at Flores, was the scene of the famous sea-fight in which Sir Richard Grenville, in command of the *Revenge*, fought a Spanish fleet in 1591: a fight immortalised by the poet Tennyson.

To the south-eastwards of the Azores lies the Madeiras. The largest member of this archipelago is the beautiful island of Madeira. All of the islands of this group are volcanic in origin although there is no activity at the present time. The two staple products of the Madeiras are wine and sugar-cane. The inhabitants are of Portuguese descent, and the archipelago, officially called Funchal, forms an integral part of the State of Portugal.

The Canary Islands, which lie some 60 miles west off the African coast between latitudes 27° and 30° N., belong to Spain. These are basaltic islands which rise steeply from the ocean bed. The soils here are productive and agriculture is profitable. Fruits, especially bananas, early vegetables such as potatoes and onions, as well as grapes and sugar-cane, are grown in abundance.

The Cape Verde Islands, which lie off the West African coast in latitude 16° N., longitude 24° W., are Portuguese. The population is mainly descendants of negro slaves. St. Vincent, the principal island of the group, is an important bunkering station for ships trading between Europe and South America, the Cape Verde Islands lying on the direct route between these two regions.

Lying on the Mid-Atlantic Ridge, almost on the Equator, are St. Paul's Rocks, a number of islets located about 500 miles east of the South American mainland. They are uninhabited and are, as to be expected, volcanic.

Ascension is a small British island lying in the South Atlantic on the Mid-Atlantic Ridge midway between the African and South American coasts. The island was discovered by a Portuguese navigator on Ascension Day in 1501. Some 700 miles to the south-east of Ascension is the Atlantic volcanic island of St. Helena.

The first permanent settlement on St. Helena was made by the British East India Company in 1659. The island was named by its Portuguese discoverer in 1502. St. Helena is best known as the place of detention of Napoleon Bonaparte from 1815 until his death in 1821. Dependencies of St. Helena include Ascension Island to the north-west and Tristan da Cunha and Gough Island on the Mid-Atlantic Ridge to the south.

Tristan da Cunha comprises three small islands which are actively volcanic and which belong to Great Britain. They lie midway between the Cape of Good Hope and the South American mainland. The islands were discovered in 1506 by the Portuguese navigator Tristao da Cunha. The British planted a garrison on the island during the time of Napoleon's detention on St. Helena, the islands being annexed by Britain in 1816. The island's population were brought to Britain following the calamitous volcanic eruption in 1961. The islanders, however, were generally unhappy in their new and strange surroundings and most of them were eager to return, and indeed did return, to their lonely Atlantic islands as soon as possible after the danger had subsided.

Gough Island is located about 200 miles to the south of Tristan da Cunha. This is the breeding-place of the giant albatross and the home of numerous seals. It was annexed by Great Britain in 1816 but has never had a permanent population.

Bouvet Island, often described as the most lonely island in the world, stands on the Mid-Atlantic Ridge in latitude 54° S. It was discovered in 1739 by the French navigator Pierre Bouvet.

Lying between the Mid-Atlantic Ridge and the shoulder of Brazil is the volcanic island of Fernando de Noronha belonging to Brazil. This serves as a place of banishment for Brazilian criminals. The island was named after its Portuguese discoverer in 1503.

To the cast of the Mid-Atlantic Ridge, and lying in the Gulf of Guinea, are several volcanic islands, chief of which is the Spanish island of Fernando Po, which lies about 20 miles off the African mainland, and the Portuguese islands of Principe and Sao Thome.

To the west of the Mid-Atlantic Ridge, in latitude 32° N., about 600 miles to the east of the North American coast, is the group of small islands known as the Bermudas. These islands are constructed of coral rock on a basaltic foundation. Their position marks the northerly limit of coral growth in the Atlantic.

The islands, noted for their beautiful scenery, are low-lying and covered with luxuriant vegetation. Birds and fish abound and the islands are favourite resorts of wealthy American tourists. They were discovered by the Spaniard Juan Bermudez from whom they take their name. The first settlement was made by the Englishman Sir George Somers in 1609, and for this reason they are sometimes known as the Somers Islands.

G

PART II

CHAPTER 7

THE DISCOVERY OF THE ATLANTIC

1. The Mediterranean Explorers and Traders

The written history of oceanic discovery began when travellers by sea first recorded their experiences—describing the places they visited and speculating on the strange things they saw. It must be borne in mind, however, that long sea voyages were made, first for exploration and then for purposes of trade, many centuries before the first written records appeared.

The earliest fragmentary evidence of voyages made in the Mediterranean takes us back to the world of the classical Greeks. It appears that the first maritime explorers of the Mediterranean region were the Phoenicians of the Levantine littoral. These sea-faring people made the coastal town of Sidon a great emporium during the middle of the second millennium B.C. Soon after Sidon had been established as a commercial centre, the city of Tyre also became famous as a great sea-port.

With the aim of extending trade and preserving it for themselves the Phoenicians established colonies at strategic places within the Mediterranean area. An important colony was set up at Carthage in about 800 B.C., and others were established in the Eastern and Western Mediterranean areas, notably in Iberia.

The date of the composition of Homer's epics is usually taken to be about 1000 B.C., but it appears that the exploits of Odysseus, the hero of the *Odyssey*, date from a very much earlier period. The vivid descriptions of harbours and sailing winds, navigation and seamanship lore, which Homer presents in his poems, make it clear that sea trading was by no means a novelty at the time.

In the period when Homer flourished the Phoenicians were the most active seafarers known to history, and Greek writers of a later period acknowledge the pilots of Sidon as masters of the Greeks in maritime matters.

We know from accounts in the *Old Testament* that the Phoenicians were great maritime traders. We are told that King Hiram of Tyre had fleets of trading vessels during the time of King Solomon who lived in Homer's day.

The Phoenicians were essentially a seafaring people. They were fearless seamen and expert navigators who ventured into regions where no other seaman would dare go. Their Tarshish ships, to which many references are made in the *Old Testament*, were the great vessels which are thought to have traded with ports lying on the Atlantic coast of North-west Europe. It seems that trade with the Tartessus region of South-west Spain, an important mining area, contributed greatly to Phoenician wealth. From Gades—believed to be Cadiz in modern Spain—the ships of Tyre and Sidon ventured northwards, and many scholars believe that the Cassiterides, from which the Phoenicians drew important tin supplies, are the Scillies or even places on the mainland of Britain.

It is evident that Phoenician seamen were at home not only in the waters of the Mediterranean and Eastern Atlantic, but also in the Red Sea, Persian Gulf and Indian Ocean. This much we know, and it is assumed that they generally went about their business with an eye to monopolizing trade. They commanded the sea trade of the Mediterranean for about 1000 years, and it is puzzling to scholars that there is an almost complete lack of records of Phoenician activities during this long period; these seafaring folk appear to have had no historians among them. It seems that they regarded their trading ventures as highly secret, and details of their routes and discoveries, and their knowledge of winds and currents and other navigational lore, which obviously had been assembled after long experience, were kept strictly to themselves.

One of the most important figures in the field of ancient geography is the fifth-century B.C. historian Herodotus. He was an acute observer and a keen and critical listener, and his remarkable history is a valuable record of his wide travels and a careful assessment of the things he saw and the reports he was given.

During his peregrinations in Egypt, Herodotus heard that in the days of King Necho a voyage of circumnavigation of the African continent had been made, under Necho's orders, by a fleet of Phoenician ships. Herodotus recorded the story although he himself was sceptical of its truth.

According to Herodotus the continent of Africa is supposed to be surrounded by sea, the discovery of this having been made by Phoenicians who were ordered by Necho to sail southwards from Egypt in the Red Sea and to return by way of the Pillars of Hercules at the western entrance to the Mediterranean. The voyage of circumnavigation of Africa, which lasted for four years, is supposed to have been undertaken during the seventh century B.C.

A hundred or so years after the legendary voyage recorded by Herodotus, in about 500 B.C., the Carthaginian Admiral Hanno made a voyage through the Pillars of Hercules and southwards along the African coast. It appears that Hanno may have reached the inner part of the Gulf of Guinea and sighted Mount Cameroon, a volcanic mountain now extinct but which may have been active in Hanno's time.

It is not unlikely that Phoenician seamen sailing in the open Atlantic discovered, by chance, some or even all of the Atlantic islands which lie off the European and African mainlands. The Azores archipelago, which lies some 800 miles from the Portuguese coast at Cape de Roca, is the westernmost group of islands in the Eastern Atlantic. A horde of Carthaginian coins found on Corvo, one of the Azores group, suggests that the Phoenicians may have visited these islands.

In Greek mythology the Isles of the Blest are located in the Atlantic Ocean outside the Pillars of Hercules. Aristotle, who flourished during the fourth century B.C., mentions a large fertile island, having perpetual summer and an abundance of all good things, located to the west of the Strait of Gibraltar. The largest island of the Madeira group is often associated with Aristotle's *Insula Fortunata*, although some scholars regard the Canaries as being the Fortunate Isles.

Ptolemy, the great geographer who flourished during the second century A.D., held that the Fortunate Isles lie at the western limit of the habitable world, and the meridian through them was used by ancient and mediaeval geographers as the datum meridian from which longitudes were measured eastwards.

At the beginning of the eighth century B.C. the great Phoenician cities of Tyre and Sidon, having reached their zenith of prosperity, began to decline. From that time onwards the Phoenician colonies turned more and more to Carthage for protection. The control of sea trade in the Eastern Mediterranean began to fall to the Greeks who had by then colonised the islands of the Aegean Sea. By the fifth century B.C. the maritime trade of Greece and her Mediterranean colonies began to surpass that of the Phoenicians in the Eastern Mediterranean.

An important voyage of discovery was made by Pytheas, of the Greek colony of Massilia, in the fourth century B.C. Unfortunately Pytheas' own account of his travels is not extant: our knowledge of this famous explorer has come down to us through the writings of others. These records are of great interest to geographers and they continue to be a source of controversy. The reason why Pytheas set out on his famous voyage is generally believed to have been to discover the trading secrets of the Phoenicians, although some think that Pytheas was a true scholar who ventured forth to seek scientific knowledge for its own sake.

Pytheas is credited with having been the first explorer to have fixed the latitudes of the places he visited. His first voyage of exploration commenced in 325 B.C. He sailed through the Pillars of Hercules and shaped his course northerly along the Atlantic coast of the Iberian peninsula. After crossing the Bay of Biscay he then, it is believed, circumnavigated the islands of Britain, during which time he sailed for six days northwards of Britain to Thule which, he reported, was on the edge of the frozen sea.

Perhaps, during a second voyage, Pytheas visited the eastern coastlands of the North Sea and it appears that in all likelihood he entered the Baltic Sea.

Speculation in connection with Pytheas' voyage has been concerned with the location of Thule, believed variously to be Iceland, the Shetland Islands, or even the coast of Northern Norway.

The places Pytheas visited were unknown to the Greeks of his time, and it seems that his explorations were isolated events so far as the Greeks were concerned. About 200 more years were to pass before Greek, and later Roman, expansion was successfully to curtail Phoenician maritime activity in the Atlantic Ocean.

The special merit of Pytheas, as far as modern geographers and historians are concerned, is that he was a skilful astronomer who used his knowledge to fix the latitudes of the places he visited. It is from his observations, which have been handed down to us by Strabo (who, incidentally, disbelieved much of what Pytheas had written about his voyages), Diodorus, and Pliny, that we are able to reconstruct Pytheas' voyages. We have also descriptions, based on Pytheas' lost account of his voyages, of tin-mining and smelting in Cornwall, and of islands where amber was to be found.

Although his work and voyages are known only through fragmentary references by later writers, Pytheas of Massilia holds a prominent place in the history of exploration. He ranks as an important explorer whose astronomical observations and geographical descriptions added significantly to man's knowledge of the Atlantic Ocean and its European coastlands and off-lying islands.

By the middle of the third century B.C., Rome, which had been growing in power since the eighth century, had become the undisputed mistress of the Italian peninsula. Although occupying the geographical and strategic centre of the Mediterranean region, Italy, hitherto, had played no active part in Mediterranean politics, but the new power was to change all this. By the second century B.C., Rome had overthrown Carthage to gain supremacy in the Western Mediterranean and had become the dominant power in the whole of the civilised Western world. And by the end of the first century A.D. the power of Rome had extended not only to the whole of the Mediterranean region but to most of Britain and to the mainland of Europe south and west of the Rhine and Danube valleys.

The Romans were great soldiers and even greater political administrators; their contributions to oceanic discovery in the Atlantic, however, were of no great significance.

Following the decline and fall of the Roman Empire a wave of Arab domination swept along the North African coastlands and spread northwards into Iberia. The splendid library at Alexandria, the centre of late Greek culture in the Mediterranean, was destroyed, and the culture of Greece and Rome was forgotten by Christian Europe until it was revived at the end of the Dark Ages.

2. *The Northern Europeans*

There is evidence that as far back as the third century A.D. piratical raids were made by Jutes and Saxons on Britain. These northern raiders, as well as the folk who lived in the coastal parts of Britain and Gaul, had the opportunity of learning what nautical knowledge the Romans had to offer them, and there is no doubt that they availed themselves of this advantage.

The voyages in the open Atlantic made by peoples of Northern Europe are the subject of many of the ancient sagas. One of the most celebrated legendary Atlantic voyages is that supposed to have been made by the Irish St. Brendan in the years between A.D. 565 and 573. Brendan set out to find the 'promised land of the Saints', usually designated St. Brendan's Isle on early maps of the Atlantic. The legend of his voyage appears, with many variations, in the early literature of the Welsh, Scottish, Bretons, Flemish and Saxons, as well as that of the Irish. It is interesting to note that the Irish of St. Brendan's time knew the Western Isles of Scotland where the first Christian church in Britain was established on the Isle of Iona by St. Columba in 563.

St. Patrick had brought Christianity to Ireland soon after the fall of Rome. It appears that many of the early Irish Christians had an urge for a life of solitude, and it became traditional for them to establish small religious communities on distant islands. Certain it is that Irish monks had reached Iceland before this island was re-discovered by the Norsemen of the ninth century.

From the eighth century onwards the Vikings, the piratical heathens of the Northlands, carried out their hostile raids on the settled peoples of North-west Europe. The Viking invasion of Ireland was accomplished in 853, at about the same time as the Norsemen had reached Iceland and had rounded the North Cape to discover the White Sea. It is not without interest to note that Othar of Helgeland, the first Norseman to voyage in the White Sea, visited the English King Alfred the Great, who recorded the discoveries of this first Arctic explorer.

According to the Norse sagas, the Viking discovery of Iceland was fortuitous, an easterly gale having blown a Faeroes-bound ship off course into the main ocean where a great island was found. On arrival, the Norse seamen found that the island had long been inhabited by a small Irish colony. Within half a century some 4000 Norse homesteads had been established on this Atlantic island, and by the year 1100 there were no less than 50,000 people of Norse and Irish mixture inhabiting Iceland.

The Viking ships may have owed their constructional origin to the galleys used by the Romans. The so-called long-ships of the Norsemen were capable of carrying about 50 men; they were propelled mainly by oars, but were equipped with a single cumbersome square sail for use with a following wind.

From Iceland the Norsemen sailed westwards and discovered Greenland and the mainland of North America.

At the beginning of the 10th century one Gunnbjorn, on a voyage to Iceland, was driven to the west of his destination by a violent east wind, and he is reported to have discovered islands well to the west of Iceland. In 982 the now-famed Eric the Red was banished from the Iceland colony. Having heard of Gunnbjorn's discovery of an earlier time, he sailed forth, legend has it, to the west to re-discover Gunnbjorn's land. Three years were to pass before Eric returned to Iceland to report his discovery of a new land which he called Greenland, a name perhaps designed to encourage folk to return with him to settle. A colony was established at Brattalid, slightly to the north of the present Julianehaab.

The Norse colony of Greenland, which prospered considerably, was Christianised by Eric's son Lief in about A.D. 1000. The same Lief Ericson is often thought to have sailed westwards from Greenland and to have explored lands on the mainland of North America, named in the sagas Vineland and Markland.

By the end of the fourteenth century the links between the colonists of Greenland and Norway, to whom the colonists swore allegiance in 1261, had been broken, and the new lands across the Atlantic slipped out of the memory of Europeans.

3. The Rise of Western European Navigation

Following on the fall of Rome, Europe entered an era, lasting for about half a millennium, of barbarism and political disorder. This long period is now called the Dark Ages. It was during this time that Irish and Viking explorers performed their striking feats of seamanship.

Following the Dark Ages, when Southern Europeans began to recover the ancient Greek and Roman cultures, maritime commerce was to blossom again in the Mediterranean region. Genoa and Venice secured great advantages from the trade that was stimulated by the Crusades, and these two City States were to become the principal centres of Mediterranean trade during the period from the end of the Dark Ages to the end of the 15th century. By the latter time the centre of gravity of sea trade had shifted westwards until it passed out of the Mediterranean entirely.

During the heyday of Genoa and Venice significant advances were made in the science of navigation: the magnetic compass had been invented, probably around the beginning of the 13th century; navigational portulan charts and sailing directions had reached a high degree of utility; and the scene was about to be set for the introduction to south-western Europeans of the application of astronomy to position-finding at sea. These improvements in navigational methods and techniques were to pave the way for the new round of explorations which were soon to be set afoot by the maritime States of Western Europe.

Astronomical methods of finding direction were used by the Phoenician and Greek navigators of the Mediterranean from earliest times. From the 13th century onwards, armed with magnetic compasses, pictorial charts and written sailing directions, the maritime traders of the Mediterranean appear to have managed amply with these navigational tools, and to have ignored the possibility of checking their positions when at sea by astronomical methods. In contrast to the navigational methods used in the enclosed waters of the Mediterranean Sea, efficient navigation in the open waters of the Atlantic Ocean required the invention of new techniques. Credit for introducing to western European navigators astronomical methods of position-finding when out of sight of land rightly belongs to the mathematicians and astronomers whom Prince Henry of Portugal had gathered around him at the onset of the Golden Age of Discovery.

By the beginning of the 15th century the western world had recovered many of the writings of the classical Greeks. In particular the works of Ptolemy on geography and cartography were to have a profound effect on the subsequent history of Western Europe.

Ptolemy who flourished at Alexandria during the middle of the second century A.D., was primarily an astronomer. In his *Geographia* he enunciated the principles of cartography and explained methods of projecting the spherical surface of a globe on to a flat surface. In addition, Ptolemy included in his *Geographia* tables of the geographical positions of all the important places of the ancient world.

Following the invention of the printing-press, Ptolemy's works appeared in the languages of Western Europe, and maps constructed on the basis of his principles and tables became widely known.

That the Earth is a sphere had been common knowledge among all thinking men from the time of Thales of Miletus, in the sixth century B.C. Eratosthenes, one of the most learned men of antiquity, made, during the second century B.C., the first scientific attempt at measuring the Earth's circumference.

Ptolemy rejected Eratosthenes' measure of the Earth's circumference, taking instead the less accurate result of Posidonius', according to whose reckoning the Earth's circumference is 18,000 miles as against Eratosthenes' 24,000 miles. In addition to this fundamental error, Ptolemy's tables of geographical positions distorted the east-west extent of the habitable world to such a degree that mediaeval geographers, who accepted Ptolemy's tables, believed that the equatorial distance across the Atlantic between Africa and Asia was considerably shorter than, in fact, it is. A voyage from the Pillars of Hercules across the waters of the Atlantic, according to Ptolemy, would be no more than 7000 miles instead of about double this distance according to Eratosthenes.

4. *Prince Henry and the Portuguese Navigators*

Little is recorded about the early maritime history of Portugal, but it is known that Lisbon and Oporto were important Portuguese trading centres as far back as the 12th century. Portugal's geographical position on the western edge of the Mediterranean world invited her to become a maritime power: with a population of little more than a million, she discovered no less than half the world within the relatively short period of a century.

The first ocean voyage undertaken by the Portuguese appears to have been made to the Canary Islands in 1341. These islands had been visited by Genoese seamen during the 13th century, and it is not unlikely that Genoese traders who had settled in Lisbon drew the attention of the Portuguese to the existence of islands far out in the Atlantic Ocean. This first Portuguese voyage of discovery appears to have been of an official nature, the ships having been supplied by the King.

The Portuguese maritime expansion during the 15th century was due to the genius of Prince Henry surnamed the Navigator. He was born in 1394, the fourth son of King John of Portugal. Henry became absorbed in problems of cosmography and geography. His haven of escape from the intrigues of men was Portugal's further-most south-westerly point where, on the rocks of Cape St. Vincent above the shores of Sagres Bay, he was able to gaze westwards across the watery wastes of the Atlantic. He pondered on the mysterious coast of Africa which ran southwards from the Strait of Gibraltar and which fronted the Atlantic waters. He had heard of the vastness of the Sahara lands of Africa and of Berber people living near the negro realms of green forests to the south of the desert. He also knew that much of the great land of Africa came under Moslem domination and that the rich trade between Asia and Europe was controlled by the Infidel. Much speculating upon the possibility of religious and economic gains led Henry to embark upon a policy of exploration and discovery of the African coastlands. There seems to be some doubt as to whether or not Henry sought to discover an Atlantic route to the treasures of the Spice Islands of Asia, but there is no doubt that his policy paved the way for this realisation.

The first voyage of exploration sponsored by Henry took place in 1419. A small expedition of two vessels under the command of João Gonçalves Zarco and Tristan Vaz Teixeria was organised to explore the West African coast and to search for the land of Guinea. The expedition came home with news of a storm which had blown them away from the land and of the consequent discovery of an island which they named Porto Santo. They had, it appears, rediscovered one of the islands of the Madeira group. Encouraged by Henry, they returned and discovered the beautiful and unin-habited Madeira, the largest island of the group.

The question arose as to the possibility of these islands belonging to the Canaries Archipelago the ownership of which, for many years, had been the subject of controversy between Spain and Portugal. Henry wanted the Atlantic islands primarily for use as bases for the exploration of the Guinea coast, and he wasted no time in colonising the islands which Zarco and Teixeira had discovered.

The Canaries, which lie relatively close to the African coast, were occupied by Moorish people. Although the islands had been raided by Spain from time to time no serious attempt had been made to plant a European colony on them until 1425. In that year Prince Henry despatched an expedition aimed at taking Gran Canaria, the largest island of the group. This attempt failed, and at the same time it incurred the wrath of Spain who thereupon set out to hamper Henry's attempts at occupation. Henry appealed ultimately to the Pope for permission to occupy the islands, and for a time the islands came under Portuguese jurisdiction. The friction between Spain and Portugal in respect of the Canaries did not come to an end until 1497 when, by the Treaty of Toledo, the Canaries were allotted to Castile.

From 1421 to 1433 Prince Henry sent expeditions to the African coast regularly, giving instructions to their commanders to double Cape Bojador. This forbidding cape, which projects from a barren coastland some 150 miles south of the Canaries traditionally marked the end of the mediaeval world. It would have been tempting providence, it seems, to have voyaged beyond Cape Bojador, on the southward side of which the ocean was thought to terminate in a horrible swamp, where the searing heat would turn white men's skin black. The mythical stories of the Sea of Darkness, which had been spread by the Arab geographers, were not the least of Henry's difficulties in attempting to persuade his captains to sail to the southwards of the Cape.

It is believed that during the year 1431 Gonçalo Velho, one of Prince Henry's captains, discovered or re-discovered the Azores. In due course islands of this group were colonised by the Portuguese. It appears that Henry had less difficulty in persuading men to sail boldly westwards into the unknown waters of the Atlantic than in persuading them to sail along the African coast south of Cape Bojador.

The year 1434 marked what is to be regarded as Henry's greatest success. In that year Gil Eanes sailed beyond the dreaded Cape. This was a deed of minor importance in itself but one which was to mark the end of mediaeval geography. Faith in geographical theories based on hearsay instead of experience was to be shaken. From that time onwards men realised that the perils to be overcome in exploring the oceans were physical, and not mythical, obstacles.

After Gil Eanes had successfully rounded Cape Bojador and returned to relate his experience, Henry found little difficulty in recruiting skilled pilots to pursue the exploration of the African coast south of Bojador. Improvements in astronomical methods were introduced at Henry's navigation school at Sagres, and increased attention was paid to ship design, all aimed to facilitate oceanic discovery. It was during this period that the first caravel was launched from Prince Henry's shipyards.

The graceful little caravel played a pioneering role in the history of oceanic discovery. Easy to manoeuvre, the caravel—Portugal's great contribution to ship design—marked a significant step forward in naval architecture, in that she was a vessel that could make steady headway to windward.

Henry had heard from captives taken during the African voyages tales of camels laden with gold which had come to Timbuktu, the desert port on the River Niger, for trans-shipment to Tunis and the Barbary coast. Where did the gold originate? Obviously far to the south of Timbuktu where negro slaves were captured by the Arabs and Berbers of the desert. Henry had heard that the land of Guinea lay outside the world of Islam and he rejoiced to learn that the negroes of that land were heathen. To bring Christianity to the pagans and perhaps discover the source of African gold were inducements enough to hold Henry to his policy of exploration.

In 1436 the Rio do Ouro was discovered by Antão Gonçalves who fetched back, in addition to slaves, the first gold dust to be brought from Africa to Portugal.

In 1444 Nuño Tristão became the first of Prince Henry's captains to see the Africa of the real negroes. In the following year Diniz Dias reached and named the western limit of the African continent Cape Verde on account of its green appearance.

Alvise da Cadamosto of Venice entered the service of Prince Henry in 1454. He is noted for his careful descriptions of his African voyages and for mapping the coastal regions more fully than had been done hitherto. Cadamosto is sometimes credited with the discovery of Cape Verde Islands. Both he and another of Prince Henry's captains claim to have discovered this archipelago sometime between 1456 and 1460.

Prince Henry the Navigator died in 1460, by which time his ships had reached as far along the African coast as Cape Palmas. The progress of oceanic discovery suffered a setback for a period immediately following Henry's death. This was temporary and the tradition was soon revived; and in 1488 the expedition of Bartolomeu Dias succeeded in rounding the southern extremity of the African continent. The promise of the discovery of India gave reason for King John of Portugal naming the southernmost stormy cape of Africa the Cape of Good Hope.

It was the experience of Dias which paved the way for the expedition of Vasco da Gama whose ships were built and equipped with the express purpose of crossing the ocean to the east of South Africa in search of a route to India. Da Gama's fleet sailed from Lisbon in July, 1497. By Christmas of the same year they had rounded the Cape and had reached land which da Gama named Natal. On May 20th, 1498, the fleet anchored off Calicut on the south-west coast of the Indian continent, and the great enterprise of discovering the Atlantic route to India had been accomplished.

After the Azores had been discovered by Velho in 1431 it was not unnatural that attempts should be made to venture westwards in search of other Atlantic islands. There had been a long-standing tradition of the existence of islands to the west of the Azores, particularly of the fabulous islands of Antillia and Brazil. This tradition was strengthened in that the inhabitants of the Azores had sometimes found trunks of trees which had been driven ashore during westerly gales, such flotsam evidently having come from lands to the west.

5. *Christopher Columbus*

Credit for having been the first southern European to cross the Atlantic is usually given to Christopher Columbus, the Genoese navigator whose expedition sponsored by Spain reached the New World in 1492. Many modern historians argue that Columbus has been unduly championed as the discoverer of the New World, the honour belonging rather to Portuguese navigators from whom Columbus learnt and whose methods he imitated.

There is strong evidence to support the view that the mediaeval discovery of America was made by a joint Portuguese-Danish expedition in 1472. The pilot of this expedition was the Portuguese navigator João Vaz Corte-Real.

Corte-Real, it appears, was rewarded by the King of Portugal with a governorship in the Azores for having made a voyage, under the King's orders, to Newfoundland, the Terra do Bacalhau of the Portuguese. It was during this voyage that it is held that Corte-Real reached the mainland coast of America. João's three sons, Vasqueanos, Gaspar and Miguel, all followed in their father's footsteps and appear to have dedicated their lives to voyaging in the North Atlantic, especially to Newfoundland, the seas off which were to become important fishing-grounds for the Portuguese.

In the year when Columbus made the first of his famous Atlantic voyages, João Fernandes made a voyage in the North Atlantic and explored the coasts of Greenland and Newfoundland, and possibly the American mainland. It was in honour of Fernandes, a farmer or *labrador* in his native Azores, that John Cabot named the mainland to the west of Greenland Labrador.

Columbus entered the scene of oceanic exploration from the outside. The exact nature of his geographical theories and their origins have been the subject of considerable academic controversy. He succeeded in enlisting the support of the Spanish monarchs Ferdinand and Isabella, who agreed to furnish him with ships and seamen for a voyage of discovery in which a search was to be made for Cathay by sailing westwards across the Atlantic.

Columbus set sail from Palos in August, 1492, for the Canaries, from which he took his departure westwards into the unknown waters of the Atlantic. Favoured with fine weather and a fair wind throughout the voyage, Columbus made a landfall on one of the outlying islands of the Bahamas 35 days after leaving the Canaries. He believed that the island, which he named San Salvador, was one of the group of which Cipangu (Japan) formed part. From San Salvador he struck out hopefully in search of the mainland of Asia. He was soon to find his fleet in the strait which we now call the Windward Passage, with the large islands of Cuba and Hispaniola to the west and east respectively. It was on the northern coast of Hispaniola that his flagship ran ashore and was wrecked, a calamity that caused him to abandon his search and decided him to return to Spain. During the homeward passage Columbus was fortunate, through having shaped a course to the northwards of that of the outward voyage, in discovering the westerly wind-belt which facilitated the homeward journey.

To follow up Columbus' discovery a second expedition was planned and this set sail from Cadiz in September, 1493. Taking part in this second expedition was a large fleet of ships and some 1200 men, together with seeds, plants, domestic animals and farming implements. The principal aim was to colonise Hispaniola with the intention of establishing a suitable base from which further explorations could be made.

During his second voyage Columbus made his landfall on the island of Dominica. He sailed northwards from here to discover the Leeward and Virgin Islands and Puerto Rico. He then ran along the south coasts of Hispaniola and Cuba and discovered the beautiful island of Jamaica.

Columbus returned to Spain in 1496. A third voyage under his command commenced in 1498. During this voyage Trinidad and the mainland of South America, in the vicinity of the mouths of the River Orinoco, were discovered. From here Columbus set course towards the north, ultimately to reach Hispaniola where he found

most of the Spanish colonists in open revolt.   In 1499, his authority
undermined, he returned to Spain as a prisoner of his successor.
The Spanish monarchs, however, restored his titles and treated him
courteously, but their confidence in him waned.   Nevertheless
Columbus made a fourth voyage, in 1502, during which new discoveries on the Caribbean mainland were made.   His search for the
Spice Islands of the East, however, had failed.   Disappointed and
with broken spirit the Admiral died in 1506.

The disappointments in Spain occasioned by the Columbian
voyages led responsible people to the realisation that the islands and
land which Columbus had discovered were considerably farther from
Asia than Columbus (who had used a circumference of the Earth
even smaller than Ptolemy's inaccurate figure) had supposed.
Exploration in the Newfoundland and Greenland region seemed to
confirm this view.   Nonetheless, voyages of discovery continued and
the great extent of the American continent, which by this time had
become known as the New World, quickly became known.

6. John Cabot

John Cabot, like Columbus, came from Genoa.   In 1484, at the
age of 34 years, he moved with his family to England.   He, like
Columbus, was imbued with the idea of reaching the East by sailing
westwards across the Atlantic.   He explained his ideas to merchants
of Bristol who supported him.   In 1497, he set sail on board the
Matthew with a complement of 18 men with the aim of discovering
the rich islands of Asia.   Some 52 days after leaving Bristol a landfall
was made on Cape Breton Island which was taken in the name of
Henry VII of England.   Cabot returned to Bristol with the news that
he had discovered the route to Cathay.   A second voyage was
hastily planned.   It was Cabot's intention originally to follow the
coast of the land he had discovered southwards as far as Cipangu,
which was believed to lie near the Equator, and which Cabot was
confident of reaching.   Before setting out on his second voyage,
however, it appears that Cabot visited Lisbon in order to enlist
experienced seamen for the voyage.   It was here perhaps that he met
João Fernandes, the farmer from the Azores, who convinced him
that the way to Cathay was northwards from Greenland.

In 1498 Cabot reached the east coast of Greenland and proceeded northwards.   He was soon to run into ice and his progress,
therefore, was severely hampered.   Ice, as well as an unwilling crew,
forced him to return southwards.   After rounding Cape Farewell at
the southern tip of Greenland he proceeded northwards on the west

side of that island, again to be impeded by ice. He thereupon proceeded southwards along the American coast to as far south as Cape Henry at the seaward entrance to our present Chesapeake Bay, in latitude 38° N. A forbidding and barren coastland, absence of an Eastern civilisation, and a diminished stock of provisions, forced Cabot to return to England. Soon after arriving home, towards the end of 1498, John Cabot died.

7. *King Manuel the Fortunate*

On Vasco da Gama's return to Spain after his memorable voyage to India, King Manuel, named the Fortunate on account of the discovery made during his reign of the sea-route to India, took steps to profit by this discovery. In the year 1500 a large expeditionary fleet was prepared for a voyage to India. This fleet, which sailed from Lisbon in March, 1500, was commanded by Pedro Álvares Cabral. A fortnight after leaving Lisbon the fleet sighted the Cape Verde Islands from which course was set south-westwards across the open Atlantic. A month later land was sighted which Cabral named Vera Cruz. This was later changed to Brazil on account of the abundance of dyewood found there.

In the year 1501, as a consequence of Cabral's report, which had been sent home before Cabral's departure from Brazil, King Manuel despatched an expedition to explore the newly-found land. This expedition of three ships, under the command of André Gonçalves, made the coast of Brazil in latitude 5° S. after which the fleet sailed southwards for some 1600 miles. The coast between Capes Sao Roque and Rio Grande do Sul was thus explored for the first time.

8. *The Naming of America*

It is probable that the Florentine explorer Amerigo Vespucci sailed with the Portuguese expedition of 1501. Vespucci gained fame through his clear geographical descriptions of the lands he explored. Many of his accounts appeared in an early 16th-century book of voyages under the title *Paesi Novamente Ritrovati*, a work which received wide popularity.

It was suggested in 1507 that the new lands across the Atlantic should be called America in honour of Vespucci. This suggestion won general approval, so that in the very year following the death of Columbus, the new lands became widely known by the name of one of Columbus' successors.

The fact that the hoped-for passage from the Atlantic to the

H

Pacific was not to be found in Central America, was established by Vasco Nuñez de Balboa who crossed the narrow Isthmus of Darien in 1513 and became the first European to sight the Pacific from its eastern shores.

The passage into the Pacific could not be found in the tropical waters of the Mexican Gulf: neither could it be found in the ice-bound seas of the North Atlantic. If indeed, it did exist, it must be sought to the south, as was the case with the passage between the Atlantic and Indian Oceans.

9. Ferdinand Magellan

Although it was the Portuguese navigator Ferdinand Magellan who first found the sea-route westwards from Europe to Asia, Magellan's expedition was sponsored, not by his native land, but by Spain. Magellan emigrated to Spain in 1517, and soon after he secured an audience with Charles V who commissioned a voyage of discovery, appointing Magellan as commander.

Magellan's fleet of five ships sailed from Seville in 1519, and the South American continent in the vicinity of Pernambuco was sighted in late November of that year. Magellan worked his way southwards and reached the estuary of the Rio de la Plata, which he examined carefully hoping to find the sought-after passage. He searched in vain and, sailing southwards, he wintered in Port St. Julian in latitude 49° S. Leaving Port St. Julian in August, 1520, he pushed southwards and discovered the eastern entrance to the strait which has, ever since, borne his name. For 38 days he guided his fleet through the narrow and tortuous 360 miles stretch of sea which separates the South American mainland from the land to the south, named by Magellan Tierra del Fuego, or the land of fire. On November 28th Magellan reached Cape Desire at the western entrance to the Magellan Strait, to sail into the ocean named by Magellan Mar del Pacifico.

Although the brave Magellan lost his life before the voyage was completed, the solitary remnant of his fleet under the command of Juan Sebastian del Cano, sailed into Seville some three years after the voyage had started with fewer than 20 men out of more than 250 who formed the original contingent.

The successful circumnavigation of the globe by Magellan and del Cano gave rise to strife between the Spanish and Portuguese. Portugal had firmly entrenched herself in the Indian Ocean after Vasco da Gama's successful voyage in 1498, and the Spanish attempt at gaining a foothold in the trade between Europe and the rich

Spice Islands of the East was to come to nought. The South American strait which Magellan had discovered, was not to be used as a regular trading route for the following two centuries. It remains to be said, however, that Magellan achieved what Columbus had set out to, but failed, to achieve. It was Magellan who was first to link Europe with Asia by a route leading westwards from Europe.

Magellan's route to the East was not practical for long after the time of its discovery. The search for a practical route to Cathay continued to be made by nations other than Spain and Portugal. The spirit of adventure fostered by these two nations spread to England, France and Holland, all three of whom embarked upon careers of oceanic discovery.

10. The English Explorers

English enterprise in overseas exploration was aroused by John Cabot who received a patent in 1496 from King Henry VII empowering him to seek unknown territories overseas. John Cabot is usually credited with the discovery of Newfoundland, England's first trans-Atlantic possession.

Following John Cabot's death in 1498 his son Sebastian, who had inherited the patent which Henry VII had granted to his father, became attached to the Society of Merchant Adventurers.

At Sebastian's suggestion a voyage in search of Cathay was planned: and, in 1553, a small fleet of three vessels set out under the captain-generalship of Sir Hugh Willoughby, with the aim of discovering a North-east passage to Cathay. Two of the ships of this fleet were wrecked and Willoughby was among those who were drowned. The remaining ship under the command of Richard Chancellor, who acted as pilot of Willoughby's fleet, reached the White Sea and entered the harbour of Archangel. Chancellor travelled overland to Moscow and received an audience with the Czar. He was instrumental in establishing trading relations by sea between England and Russia.

Following Chancellor's return to England several other voyages were made in attempts to discover a North-east passage. In one expedition, led by Stephen Brough, the entrance to the Kara Sea was reached.

It was in the reign of Elizabeth I that the great flowering of England's overseas activity took place. Prominent among the promoters of maritime adventure was Richard Hakluyt, whose collection of records of English voyages, together with that of his worthy successor Samuel Purchas, remains to this day the principal source of information relating to the early navigations undertaken by Englishmen.

Failure to discover a practical North-east passage to the fabulous East led to further attempts being made to seek a North-west passage. In this connection Martin Frobisher led the way in 1576. He commanded three voyages to Greenland, only the first of which was a voyage of discovery. The second and third were made in consequence of Frobisher's belief that he had discovered a rich source of gold. These voyages failed completely in their purpose.

In 1585 John Davis was engaged to lead an expedition of discovery by London merchants, principal of whom was William Sanderson. In all, Davis commanded three voyages of discovery in Arctic regions, during the third of which he reached latitude 72° N. in Baffin Bay, naming the bluff in the vicinity on the Greenland coast 'Sanderson His Hope of a North-west Passage'.

In 1607, Henry Hudson was despatched on a voyage of discovery in which he explored the east coast of Greenland and Spitsbergen, reaching latitude $80\frac{1}{2}°$ N. In a later voyage, in which Hudson sailed for the Dutch, he discovered the American river which now bears his name.

The most successful northern voyage of the 17th century commenced in 1616, when the tiny bark *Discovery* of only 35 tons burden, sailed from England under Robert Bylot as Master and William Baffin as pilot. During this voyage the head of Baffin Bay was discovered. Two whole centuries were to pass before the so-called 'north waters' of Baffin Bay were again to be explored.

The maritime enterprise of England during the Elizabethan times was aimed primarily at discovering a northern passage to Cathay, but voyages to Guinea and to the West Indies were also undertaken. In 1577, Sir Francis Drake successfully circumnavigated the globe. During Drake's celebrated voyage, his small ship, whose name *Pelican* was changed to *Golden Hind*, was driven southwards after having negotiated the Magellan Strait, and the passage between Tierra del Fuego and the Antarctic continent was discovered. This passage still bears the name of the first Englishman to circumnavigate the globe.

After entering the Pacific, Drake proceeded northwards along the American coast to search in vain for a passage into the Atlantic. He appears to have reached the latitude of San Francisco, in the commodious harbour of which he refitted his ship.

Thomas Cavendish emulated Drake's voyage in 1586 and so did Richard Hawkins in 1594.

During the 16th and 17th centuries tremendous progress was

achieved in the art of navigation largely as a result of the maritime activity of the period. New instruments were invented to facilitate astronomical navigation, the most significant advance made in this direction being the invention of the quadrant by John Davis, the Arctic explorer. During the 17th century the Dutch became pre-eminent in map- and chart-making.

In the closing year of the 17th century the English Astronomer-Royal, Edmund Halley, undertook a scientific voyage as a result of which the first magnetic variation chart of the globe was produced.

11. The French and Dutch Explorers

At the start of the 16th century the French engaged in maritime activity, particularly in the North-west Atlantic region. In 1524 the French King Francis I engaged the Florentine explorer Giovanni da Verazzano to undertake a voyage of discovery to the coast of North America. Ten years later Jacques Cartier commanded an expedition designed to follow up the work of Verazzano. During this expedition, and during succeeding voyages, Cartier discovered the large island of Anticosti and the Gulf of and River St. Lawrence. The great river of North America was explored, Cartier ascending the river to the rapids near the site of present Montreal. A French colony ultimately was planted in Arcadia, the land discovered by Cartier, but attempts at establishing a colony in Florida at about the same time were successfully thwarted by the Spanish.

The French Arcadian colony was established in 1611 at Quebec largely through the efforts of Samuel Champlain who was installed as the first governor of the new colony.

The Dutch, during the latter part of the 16th century emulated the English exploratory voyages in search of the North-east passage. Trade between the Dutch and the Russians was established in 1578. The famous Dutch cosmographer Peter Plancius induced the merchants of Amsterdam to attempt to seek a North-east passage, which had been found to be impracticable through the ice-encumbered Kara Sea, to the north of the large island of Novaya Zembla. A voyage was planned and the expeditionary fleet sailed from Texel in 1594 under the command of Willem Barents. The sought-for passage was not found but, in a subsequent voyage in 1596, Spitsbergen was discovered and explored by Barents.

The Dutch were active in gaining a foothold in the Indian Ocean and by 1616 the Dutch East India Company had nearly 40 ships in service and over 3000 troops stationed at strategic places in the East Indian islands.

A Dutch expedition under Jacob le Maire and Jan Schouten sailed from Texel in 1615 to establish a trade-route between Europe and Asia by way of the Magellan Strait. During this voyage the first passage from the Atlantic into the Pacific through the Drake Passage was accomplished, and the southerly cape of Tierra del Fuego was named Horn after the town in West Friesland from which Jan Schouten hailed.

12. *The Exploration of the Southern Ocean*

The voyages of Captain James Cook are sometimes held to have been the last of the great voyages of ocean discovery. Cook's voyages of geographical discovery marked the culmination of the Golden Age of Discovery initiated by the Portuguese at the close of the 14th century. By Cook's time most of the American and African coastlands of the Atlantic had been mapped. The North-east and North-west Passages, however, had not been discovered and considerable doubt existed as to the nature of the southern polar region. The traditional view of the Antarctic was that of the existence of a large land-mass named by the Ancients *Terra Australis*. During the 18th century the concept of a great southern continent gave way to that of a great southern ocean. It was Captain Cook who finally demonstrated the existence of a southern ocean which extended completely around the globe. Cook had circumnavigated the globe in the waters of the southern seas and had crossed the Antarctic Circle in doing so: if a southern continent did exist, its limits were well to the southwards of those hitherto supposed.

The first planned attempt at discovering the south land of Antarctica is supposed to have been made by Pierre Bouvet of the French East India Company. Bouvet sailed southwards in 1739 and navigated his ship through some 48° of longitude in an ice-encumbered sea along the parallel of latitude 55° S. An important discovery made during this voyage was the island, now named after its discoverer, in latitude 54° S.

Cook, in 1772, in command of the *Resolution*, searched unsuccessfully for Bouvet Island. It was during this voyage that Cook exploded the myth of a southern habitable continent.

The famous Russian explorer Fabian von Bellingshausen supplemented the geographical discoveries of Cook in the Southern Ocean during a memorable voyage in 1819.

Soon after Cook's voyages, sealing expeditions to Antarctic waters were organised by the British. In 1819 William Smith, whilst in command of a sealer, sighted land to the south of Cape

Horn in latitude 62° 40′ S. In 1823, James Wedell, in command of the sealer *Jane*, reached the parallel of 74° 15′ S., the highest latitude then attained, in the sea which now bears his name. Three years later Captain John Biscoe discovered the mainland of Antarctica in longitude 49° E., and later again, in 1832, Biscoe discovered the Grahamland peninsula of Antarctica.

CHAPTER 8

ECONOMIC RESOURCES OF THE ATLANTIC

1. Introduction

It is accepted generally by biologists that the salt sea provided the environment in which the earliest life on Earth was cradled. And certain it is that without the beneficent ocean, life on the continents would be utterly impossible. The ocean is the Earth's great water reservoir—the source of the life-giving atmospheric moisture on which all land-plants and animals depend for their development and survival. Without the seas the land surfaces of the globe would be lifeless deserts.

The waters of the ocean also provide a great natural thermo-statically-controlled heat reservoir. This releases warmth to the atmosphere in the temperate regions during winter, thereby allevi-ating the cold which would otherwise make human life virtually impossible in these regions.

The ocean in its role as a huge reservoir of life-giving water and heat is man's most important natural resource. But in many other ways the ocean provides for the needs of man. It provides the least expensive mode of transportation, facilitating the movement of food and other supplies between the principal centres of the world's population: and it provides a playground for the increasing number of people who have learnt to enjoy the several forms of water-sport, such as sailing and motor-boating, and for those who delight in holidays by the sea. The ocean also provides, or could provide other valuable resources for the well-being of mankind. Let us examine the more important of these resources in some detail.

2. Fresh Water from the Sea

Not only for domestic uses, which in large urban centres creates a problem of immense magnitude, but also for almost every industrial activity, the plentiful supply of fresh water on tap is of great import-ance. Hitherto this supply has been obtained from land sources, particularly from lakes and streams and from wells sunk into the ground. With the ever-growing demand for fresh water, especially for industrial needs, the time is fast approaching when the question of fresh-water supply, in countries such as most of those of North-west Europe, whose economies are industrially-based, is becoming critical

In certain places, particularly certain oceanic islands such as Ascension Island in the Atlantic, and settlements located on desert coasts, the distillation of fresh water from the sea is carried out on a relatively large scale. On the other side of the Atlantic, Key West in Florida is the first United States' city to obtain its fresh water supply from the ocean by means of a large distillation plant.

The process of distilling fresh water from the sea is costly and wasteful of large quantities of energy, and much research is today being conducted on attempts at discovering methods of obtaining fresh water from the sea more economically than has hitherto been possible. The most promising technique of reducing the cost of distillation of sea water is to link the process with that of the extraction of valuable minerals from the sea, or with the process of generating electricity as has been done in some nuclear power-plants where sea-water distillation is carried out using heat from the atomic processes involved in the plants. Schemes for impounding tidal waters in estuaries, so that the initially-salt-water is gradually converted to fresh-water, have been proposed for Solway Firth in Scotland, Morecambe Bay off the coast of Lancashire, as well as for other places. In time, sophisticated barrage schemes, such as those proposed, will doubtless be helping significantly to solve the growing problem of fresh-water supply.

3. Tidal Energy

The periodic rising and falling of sea-level, the tide, is very pronounced in coastal waters as compared with that in the deep oceanic waters. The harnessing of the energy associated with the tide has, until recent times, been all but neglected. Greatest tidal ranges in the world are to be found in the northern parts of the Bay of Fundy, where tidal ranges of as much as 50 feet are experienced. It happens, also, that in many places in North-west Europe, particularly in the English and Bristol Channels, tidal ranges are considerable. Industries based near these localities might well be served by electrical power produced from the energy of the large-amplitude oscillations of the sea-level. As long ago as 1933 a plan was proposed for a barrage to be constructed in the Severn Estuary, in the upper part of the Bristol Channel, with the express purpose of harnessing tidal energy, but the scheme has not yet reached fruition. The French, however, have succeeded in constructing a barrage in the

Rance Estuary near St. Malo on the Brittany coast. This barrage was designed to feed some 500 million kilowatt hours per annum into the French electrical grid system. The dam in the Rance scheme houses a number of reversible turbines capable of being operated by both the ebb and the flood tidal streams.

4. *Pollution of the Sea*

The ocean has provided man with a huge waste receptacle into which he has, often thoughtlessly, dumped sewage and industrial refuse. Within recent decades several nations have invested capital in atomic power stations so that the increasing demands for electrical energy may be met. From the earliest stage in this development scientists have turned to the sea to assist them for a variety of reasons. First, the sea has been used to provide the vast quantities of water necessary for cooling purposes; second, it has been used as a source of deuterium, or heavy water, which is used in nuclear reactors; and third, it has acted very conveniently as a dumping-ground for radio-active waste material produced in the processes of converting nuclear energy into electrical energy. The dangers related to the disposal of this waste material are not yet fully appreciated, and studies associated with atomic waste are now proceeding at international level with the aim of regulating its disposal. It is of interest to note that at the present time man-produced radio-activity resulting from nuclear fall-out from atomic explosions can be isolated in relatively small samples of sea-water taken from any part of the ocean.

As well as impressive programmes for the creation of nuclear power-stations at coastal locations, some nations possess, or have plans to produce, nuclear-powered surface-ships and submarines, and these craft have brought additional problems related to sea pollution.

The pollution of the sea by petroleum has steadily increased since the advent of the oil-tanker and the internal-combustion engine. This careless activity of man has resulted in the loss of innumerable marine animals and sea-birds and the pollution of hundreds of miles of beaches, especially around the coasts of North-west Europe.

The coastal location of large plants associated with oil refining, the petro-chemical industry, metal refining and numerous other industries, has resulted in the dumping of considerable quantities of industrial effluent into the sea, this often having had disastrous effects on local fish populations and offshore fisheries. Another frightening source of pollution in the sea stems from toxic residues from pesticides which are washed from the soil, ultimately to reach the sea by way of rivers and streams.

It is of great importance that the waters of the ocean and its peripheral seas provide mankind with a valuable food supply. In addition the ocean is an enormous storehouse of metals and minerals which will, in the future, be exploited on a large scale to provide for the world's industrial activities. It is only within recent decades that men have come to the realisation that the ocean is a repository of tremendous resources of food and mineral wealth which must be exploited sensibly and efficiently to meet the increasing needs of a rapidly expanding world population. Let us now discuss the ocean in its role as a provider of food for mankind.

5. *Food from the Atlantic*

The water of the ocean provides sustenance for a vast host of marine plants and animals which live out their lives immersed in this life-giving medium. Sea-water is a very complex liquid from which about 60 of the 90 or so elements have been extracted. Some of these elements are found in solution in sea-water in relatively large proportions, whereas others appear as mere traces. In addition to inorganic matter in solution, sea-water contains suspended organic material, the presence of this making it impossible for sea-water to be created artificially.

The waters of the ocean are in a state of continual motion to such a degree that the relative proportions of dissolved minerals are almost identical for samples drawn from any part of the sea. Dissolved minerals in sea-water, and the natural aeration of the surface layer of the sea through which sunlight can penetrate, give rise to conditions which are ideal for the growth of the abundant plant-life to be found in the sea.

Plants, it may be remembered, are the only life forms capable of transforming energy in the form of solar radiation into chemical energy of organic matter. The process by which this is possible is known as photosynthesis, in which plants form carbohydrates from carbon-dioxide and water through the agency of sunlight acting on a substance, peculiar to all plants, known as chlorophyll. Photo-synthesis is possible only if sunlight is available, so that in the sea plants exist only in the uppermost layer, the thickness of which is limited to that through which sunlight, sufficient for the process, can penetrate. This thickness varies with the altitude of the Sun, the length of daylight, and the turbidity of the water.

The fact that photosynthesis is possible only through the agency of plants makes plant life the basis of all animal life, in the ocean as well as on land. Animal life in the sea tends to be most abundant in localities where plant-life is most plentiful. It is for this reason that the important fisheries of the world, at the present time, are to be found in continental shelf areas, where the water depth allows plants to exist at all levels.

Hitherto man's attitude to sea fisheries has been primarily one of hunting. Now the primitive methods of hunting animals on land, to provide for the hunter and his family, are relatively inefficient and unproductive compared with the rearing of livestock by efficient husbandry of farmland. So it is in respect of the sea. The time is now approaching for the large-scale exploitation of the ocean's food resources by systematic and scientific methods which will in no way jeopardise the natural balance of marine biological activities.

Most fish are abundantly prolific: the eggs produced by a single female fish, in most cases, are in the order of hundreds of thousands per spawning season. At all stages in their existence, however, fish are attacked by innumerable enemies to such a degree that not more than a fraction of one per cent of the eggs produced by fish ever become mature animals.

Up to the present time the philosophy of exploiting the food resources of the sea, with the possible exception of certain edible molluscs, which are included in the so-called shellfish, has not advanced beyond the primitive level of hunting or gathering. The practice of fishing, even in this scientific age, is still governed largely by tradition and the personal experiences of fishermen. Moreover, of the numerous species of marine animals only a relatively small number enter into the diets of most fish-consuming people. In view of the tremendous potential in fish production, a dream of many marine biologists is the large-scale introduction of successful methods of farming the sea, a process now known as aquaculture.

To promote the efficient exploitation of the sea, scientists are devoting their attention increasingly to the intensive study of fish and their habits and habitats. The task of tracing the relationships between fish and their environment with reference to food supply, the presence of predators, and the several oceanographical factors, including sea temperature and salinity, is extremely difficult: but the task has to be faced if the seas are to serve the growing needs of the Earth's increasing population.

In addition to a wide variety of fish, the harvest of the sea includes many edible molluscs such as oysters, clams, cockles and mussels, and a wide range of gasteropods, including winkles and whelks and other forms of sea-snails. In some parts of the world edible sea-weeds are gathered, these being used to add variety and interest to the human diet. The sea is the home of several species of mammals, including the whale and the seal. These animals could provide important food resources for mankind if they are exploited thoughtfully with the view to conservation and not merely as part of a robber economy which hitherto has, unfortunately, been the case.

Before discussing the food resources of the Atlantic we shall discuss briefly the processes involved in the life-cycles of certain forms of marine life.

Perhaps the fundamental form of life in the waters of the ocean is the plankton. The name plankton, which is derived from the Greek meaning to wander, is given to the innumerable species of plants and animals which are sustained and supported by the waters of the ocean, and whose power of controlling their movements are non-existent or developed to a degree so small that they are too feeble to resist the motions of the sea.

Most plankton are microscopic and unicellular, although some species, including certain types of so-called jelly-fish, attain large proportions. Included in the plankton are the larvae of fish and other marine life-forms in the early stages of their development.

The plant- or phyto-plankton of greatest abundance is the microscopic diatom of which there are thousands of species. These tiny plants have the ability to extract silicon and oxygen from sea-water in order to form a complex cell-case of transparent silica. Every diatom is an individual cell whose siliceous cell container is formed of two parts or valves which fit together like a tiny pill-box and its lid. Diatoms reproduce by a process of cell division whereby the two valves of the cell-case separate, each carrying with it a half of the living cell material. After division each new cell secretes a new valve to complete its cell-case or frustule. The reproducing rate of diatoms is very rapid: their numbers, discounting natural loss, increasing in geometrical progression. It has been estimated that from a single specimen no fewer than a thousand million diatoms are produced in a month.

Diatoms flourish in the waters of high latitudes and off cold-water coasts. Within the Atlantic their distribution is confined to Arctic waters and to a broad belt of Antarctic waters, as well as to a limited region off the South-west coast of Africa in the vicinity of Walvis Bay.

Prominent amongst the phyto-plankton are the tiny plants which collectively form the flagellates. These take their name from whip-like appendages by the action of which they are able to prevent themselves from sinking by propelling themselves upwards against the force of gravity. Notable among these tiny plants are the dino-flagellates. These are responsible for much of the luminescence of the sea, the species Noctiluca being particularly brilliant in this respect.

The diatoms and flagellates between them account for the greater proportion of the microscopic plant-life of the ocean waters. They form, therefore, the basis of all other marine life.

Plant-life in the ocean undergoes a cyclic period of growth and development in a way similar to that of land-plants. This cycle is most prominent in temperate and high latitudes where seasonal changes in temperature are most conspicuous. The growth of marine plant-life, and indeed that of animal life too, is partly dependent upon a plentiful supply of nutrients. It is interesting to consider how these become available to serve the needs of marine plant-life.

We have noted that by the process of photosynthesis, which can take place only in the photozoic zone of the ocean, plants are able to extract inorganic material from sea-water, and to transform it into organic material. Now it is important to realise that some mechanism must exist whereby the remains of organic life can be changed back into inorganic material to be made available for the processes involved in photosynthesis by plants. Much of the organic material from dead plants and animals gravitates towards the sea-bed. In the presence of oxygen and bacteria within the sea dead organic material decays and is transformed into inorganic minerals. It follows that whereas inorganic matter is transformed into organic material near the sea surface, the reverse process takes place largely at levels below the photozoic zone. The vertical circulation of the ocean is, therefore, of vital importance in returning the necessary nutrient salts from the lower regions of the ocean, where bacterial action is most active, to the upper regions where plants are able to extract them from the sea.

Following winter, the surface waters of the ocean become warmed from the increasing daily amount of heat received from the Sun. There comes a time in early spring when the increasing amounts of warmth and sunlight provide conditions favourable for an outburst of phyto-planktonic activity. The relatively small number of microscopic plants which have survived from the previous season begin to multiply at a prodigious rate so that the surface layer of the sea soon becomes densely packed with thousands of millions of tiny plants which sometimes discolour the sea and which foul the nets of fishermen.

As the days lengthen and summer arrives, the warmth of the surface layers of the sea results in decreased density. This, in turn, tends to inhibit the upward-moving currents necessary to rejuvenate the surface waters of the nutrient salts necessary for planktonic activity. These waters eventually become depleted of their content of nutrient salts and the phyto-plankton thereupon discontinue multiplying.

The flagellates, in contrast to most forms of phyto-plankton, require only relatively small amounts of nutrients, so that their reproducing activity persists for longer than that of diatoms and other rarer phyto-plankton.

The plant-plankton provide sustenance for innumerable animals, or zoo-plankton, so that following each outburst of phyto-planktonic activity there is an upsurge in the population numbers of the tiny animals which thrive, or graze, on the plants, or grass, of the ocean waters. Larger marine animals rely on the zoo-plankton for their food supplies and these, in turn, provide—albeit unwillingly—for the needs of their attackers, predatoriness being a characteristic feature of almost every form of marine animal life.

Perhaps the most prominent of the tiny animals which graze the plants of the ocean are the minute shrimp-like crustaceans called copepods. Having a life-cycle of only about 10 days copepods reproduce profusely and quickly. In their turn they make the abundance of marine plants available to other animals so that a plentiful supply of plant-plankton gives rise to an abundance of a variety of marine animals.

Most of the zoo-plankton are unicellular animals belonging to the phylum protozoa. An important sub-group of this phylum is the order foraminifera, or the forams as they are usually called. Most members of this order secrete shells of calcium carbonate.

The most prolific and abundant of marine foraminifera are members of the genus globigerina, which comprises numerous species. The discarded shells of these tiny animals cause no less than half the floor of the Atlantic to be covered with globigerina ooze, a finely-divided calcareous oceanic deposit made up almost entirely of the tiny globular shells of globigerinae.

In parts of the Atlantic Ocean, especially south of the Equator, a prominent marine animal is the tiny gasteropod of the phylum mollusca belonging to the genus pteropoda. Most species of pteropoda are found in warm waters whose depths are less than about 150 fathoms. They secrete calcareous shells which, on the death of the animals, fall to the sea-bed where, in some parts of the South Atlantic they help to form a characteristic sea-bottom deposit known as pteropod ooze.

Most, if not all, fish undertake seasonal breeding or spawning migrations. The sardines of the eastern North Atlantic migrate between the waters off the Portuguese coast and those of the northern part of the Bay of Biscay. The several species of herring which inhabit the seas of North-west Europe perform vertical migrations.

Herring breed in relatively cold coastal waters. During the onset of summer the herring leave the warming surface of the seas of North-west Europe for the cooler waters at depth on the European continental slopes. Later in the year, when the surface waters become cool at the onset of, and during, winter, the herring rise to spawn.

Perhaps the most splendid example of fish migration is that of the eels which are common in the rivers of Britain and the near continent. In the autumn of each year the adult eels forsake the European rivers and set out to make their way, heading against the North Atlantic drift current, to the Sargasso Sea where, after spawning, they die. The eggs and larvae are carried eastwards to Europe by the same current against which the adult eels fought their way when coming to the spawning-grounds, taking about three years to complete the journey. On arrival in the rivers of Europe the young eels change into elvers; and, after spending several years in the fresh waters of the rivers, during which time they grow to attain lengths of three or four feet, they leave the rivers for their Atlantic odyssey.

The herring, like the sardine, sprat, mackerel and pilchard, are examples of shoaling fish which are caught largely by means of drift-net fishermen. Other fish of commerce, such as the cod, hake, halibut, plaice and sole, are described as demersal fish, by which is meant that they inhabit the waters lying close to the sea-bed and are, therefore, bottom-feeders. Demersal fish are caught from trawlers or long-line fishermen.

The nets of a drift-net fishing-vessel, which hang like a curtain from a hawser or warp which is supported at the sea surface by cork or glass floats, may extend for three or four miles from the vessel which lies to leeward of the nets and which drifts downwind. The net is designed to intercept fish of large size who, in their attempt to pass through, are caught by their gills. Periodically the net is hove in so that the trapped fish may be landed on board the drifter and stowed away in the fish-hold in ice ready for market.

In contrast to the drift-net fisherman the trawler fisherman drags an open-mouthed net or trawl along the sea-bed close astern of the trawler, so that an attempt is made for the net to be brought to the fish. The mouth of the trawl is kept open by means of kite-like otter boards. After heaving the trawl on board the closed end of the net, known as the cod end, is opened to allow the catch to fall on deck ready for gutting and subsequent stowing.

The process of long-lining involves baiting a large number of hooks which are secured by thin, but strong, lines to the heavier fishing-line. After shooting, the line is left for a time before hauling in. The Portuguese dorymen who fish from larger parent ships on the Grand Banks of Newfoundland still engage in long-line fishing, but this activity is rapidly declining in the face of more efficient and less arduous fishing methods.

The principal fishing-grounds of the Atlantic are confined to the North Atlantic and Arctic waters. The eastern part of the North Atlantic, extending from the coastal waters of Morocco northwards to the Norwegian North Cape, abound in shoaling and demersal fish. Among the former, herring, sprat, mackerel, sardine and pilchard are taken in large quantities and sold for immediate consumption as well as to local canning factories. Of the demersal fish, cod, halibut, plaice, hake and sole, from the waters resting on the North-west European continental shelf, are the more popular sea-fish served on the dining-tables of Europe. Marine molluscs of great diversity are also of considerable local importance.

Most of the nations of North-west Europe have long histories associated with fishing activities in European waters. Fishing has often been held to have prepared the way for sea-trade. In the Middle Ages the salting and marketing of Baltic herring in southern Sweden were thriving commercial activities and the Hanseatic League is often regarded as having gained much of its early power by acquiring and controlling the herring fisheries of this region. The rise of the Dutch as the pre-eminent maritime nation of the 17th century was closely related to their monopoly of the fishing-grounds of the North Sea.

The Norwegians normally catch a volume of fish per year exceeding that of any other European nation, although the value of their annual catch is almost the lowest of that of the fishing nations of North-west Europe. Herring is the predominant fish of the Norwegian catch, but the difficulties of marketing or salting or canning are so great during the relatively short season that much of the catch is reduced to fish-meal for industrial uses. Cod accounts for a relatively small volume compared with that of the total catch, but its value is relatively large. The seas in the vicinity of the Lofoten Islands are the favourite cod-fishing-grounds worked by Norwegian trawlers who operate mainly from the northern Norwegian ports of Tromso and Hammerfest. The principal ports

I

associated with the Norwegian herring fisheries are Bergen and Stavanger in southern Norway.

The Danish fishing industry is particularly important to Denmark. Her catches of eel and plaice are marketed fresh in the densely-populated parts of nearby Germany.

Some 90 per cent of the working population of the Faeroe Islands gain their livelihood from fishing. Faeroese fishermen work chiefiy in the waters off Iceland and Greenland.

Since the end of the Second World War West Germany has developed very important and efficient fishing fleets. France also has a large fishing fleet which engages in fishing in the open Atlantic as well as in the English Channel and North Sea. The Spanish and Portuguese also have important fishing fleets, the chief catch being sardine. The economy of Iceland is geared essentially to her important fishing industry.

The British fishing industry, as was the case with that of other North-west European nations, was influenced greatly by the improved communications associated with the rise of the railway era. From that time onwards the innumerable small fishing villages of Britain fell into a state of decline and the industry concentrated more and more on a relatively small number of fishing-ports, including Hull, Grimsby, Aberdeen and Lowestoft on the east coast, and Fleetwood and Milford Haven on the west coast of Britain. With the centralisation of the British fishing industry fresh fish for immediate consumption found its way to the remotest country towns and villages.

The more delectable fish caught in the fishing-grounds of the North Sea, Irish Sea and English Channel, such as sole, plaice and hake, have gradually given way to less-favoured cod, this reflecting the change that has come about in the British fishing industry since the advent of railways and bigger and better-equipped trawlers. The fisheries of the northern waters in the vicinity of Iceland and Spitsbergen are the favourite fishing-grounds of large numbers of British trawlers most of which are operated from the North Sea ports of Hull and Grimsby. About two-thirds, by weight, of the fish consumed in Britain are caught in the cold Arctic waters to the north of Norway. A recent development in fishing is the quick-freezing of fish, the process being carried out on board the fishing-vessel itself. The fish are cleaned and filleted—often by means of elaborate and expensive machinery—and then wrapped and packed ready for sale in the super-markets of the large towns.

Despite the vigorous fishing activities of the nations of Europe, fish and other food from the sea accounts for not more than about four per cent of the diet of Europeans. The people of Britain for example consume on average not more than 40 lbs. per capita per annum.   Compared with the amount of protein obtained from the meat of cattle, sheep and pigs, in the European diet, that from fish is very small indeed.   One may well wonder, in view of the increasing protein requirements for the world's growing population, what these relative amounts will be for the human inhabitants of the Earth in the generations to come.

In the North-western Atlantic enormously productive fishing-grounds exist in the banks lying off the coasts of North-east Canada and Newfoundland and New England.   The fishing-grounds in the open seas in these localities are available to all nations; and British, French and other European fishermen work here in company with those of Canada and the United States.

The principal varieties of fish caught in the fishing-grounds of the North-west Atlantic are cod, mackerel, hake, haddock and herring.   A fish similar to herring called menhaden is also caught in large quantities off the eastern coast of the United States between Long Island and South Carolina.

Newfoundland fisheries are engaged almost entirely in cod fishing.   Important cod-drying and curing factories have been established in Newfoundland which exports large amounts of salt- and dried-cod to the Latin countries of Europe, especially Spain, Portugal and Italy.   These commodities also find a ready market in the West Indies and parts of South America.

In the South Atlantic fishing is of relatively small importance. The waters off the South-west African coast have considerable potential, but these waters have not yet been exploited on anything like the scale of the North Atlantic fisheries.

6. Watling in the Atlantic

The whaling industry flourished in the North Atlantic during the 18th and 19th centuries, and even today whaling plays a big part in the economy of the Faeroe Islands.   Towards the end of the 19th century signs of depleting stocks in northern waters induced whaling companies to seek new whaling-grounds in the waters of the Southern Ocean.   Since 1904, when the first large whaling expedition to Antarctica was made, whaling has been centred at stations in the southern hemisphere.   In 1922 the first whale factory-ship was commissioned, and this marked an important epoch in the history of the whaling industry.

A modern whale factory-ship has a capacity of about 30,000 tons of whale products.   She is attended by a small fleet of from six to nine smaller whale catchers who supply captured animals for the factory ship to process. During the whaling season, which lasts from December to March, the slaughter of whales takes place on a large scale and, in spite of international regulations regarding recommended quotas for each of the nations who participate in whaling, the numbers of whales decrease year by year, and there is a great fear that these mighty marine animals may soon become extinct.

The chief whaling areas of the South Atlantic are off the South-west African coast, in the waters off the Falkland Islands, and in the Ross Sea of Antarctica. Norwegians, Japanese and Russians, are the principal whaling peoples of the present time and their whaling fleets operate during the season from bases in South Georgia and the South Orkney Islands. The processing of whale products is the principal industrial activity of the Falkland Islanders.

7. Mineral Resources

The recent advances in marine geology and geophysics have been stimulated in part by the growing demand for the raw materials of industry. Until recent times the mineral ores and natural fuels which feed the world's industrial machinery were extracted almost entirely from the rocks of the continent. In recent times, however, there has been a growing awareness of the vast industrial potential of the rocks which form the sea-bed, the sediments which rest on the sea-bed, and the sea itself.

To exploit the treasures of the sea and its bed on a scale sufficiently large to make it economically worthwhile requires intensive study of the marine environment. This has brought about the invention and introduction of sophisticated instruments designed for measuring and investigating the several factors of the marine environment. By means of improved echo sounders it is now possible to produce accurate bathymetric maps from which the exact topography of the sea-bed may be seen. Improved seismic and gravimetric methods have enabled scientists to estimate accurately the thicknesses and relative disposition of the strata which form the uppermost layer of the sea-bed and those of the sediments which repose upon it. Other geophysical advances, made in relatively recent time, enable scientists to measure the radioactivity and magnetic condition of the rocks which form the sea-bed, as well as the rate of flow of heat from the solid Earth to the lower layers of the ocean waters.

The exploration of the sea-bed by visual examination is now

possible, thanks to the genius of those who have invented deep submersibles, such as the bathyscaph—the brainchild of the brilliant Swiss scientists, father and son, Professor Auguste, and Dr. Jacques, Picard.   Research is proceeding to provide new ways in which men can remain submerged for long periods of time, and in this connection the name of the French Commandant Jacques Cousteau is brought to mind.

It is estimated that there are some 330 million cubic miles of sea-water in the oceans, and that there are, on average, about 166 million tons of dissolved material in each cubic mile of sea-water. In each cubic foot of sea-water there is on average some 35 ounces of so-called salt.

Marine plants and animals extract from sea-water the minerals they require for their organic processes in a very efficient manner. Were such methods of extraction available to the analytical chemist it is not unlikely that every naturally-occurring element could be found in the sea, water being the universal solvent.   Up to the present time chemists have successfully recovered from sea-water some 60 of the 90 or so elements.

The most abundant salt in sea-water is sodium chloride or common salt.   Sodium and chlorine together constitute about 85 per cent of dissolved material in sea-water.   Common salt is a valuable raw material of the chemical industry, it being the basis of the manufacturing of soda.   It is also an important domestic product being used extensively in food preservation and preparation.

At places where climatic conditions are favourable men have, for generations, evaporated sea-water in order to obtain common salt, and even today sea-salt is obtained in large quantities by solar evaporation in parts of the Mediterranean and many other places. In cool places, where the solar evaporation method of extracting salt from sea-water is impracticable, a freezing process is sometimes employed.   This is a method widely used in Sweden and the U.S.S.R.

When sea-water is cooled to a temperature below about $-4°$ C., ice, consisting almost of pure H_2O, is formed.   If the remaining brine is removed, the ice, on melting, produces fresh water.   To produce salt a succession of freezing stages is carried out after the brine is sufficiently concentrated to be evaporated economically by the application of artificial heat.

The dissolved constituents of sea-water do not exist in solution in their normal molecular state of electrical neutrality: they appear in the form of ions, these being parts of atoms or molecules having either positive or negative charges.   Chlorine, for example, appears as a chloride ion, this making up more than half, some 55 per cent of, the solid material in solution in sea-water. Sodium, which is next to chlorine in order of relative abundance, appears as a positive ion. The sodium ion accounts for 30 per cent of the dissolved material in sea-water. The elements chlorine, sodium, sulphur and magnesium, are not used to any great extent by marine life. The remaining elements collectively account for such a small proportion of the total mass of the dissolved material that the extraction by marine plants and animals of the minerals they need does not materially affect the relative proportions of the dissolved constituents of sea-water.

Although the ocean is a repository of a vast store of valuable metals, its value as a source of any particular metal depends largely upon the cost of extraction, particularly in comparison with the cost of extraction from continental ore supplies. The fact that there is more than sufficient gold in the sea to make every person on Earth a millionaire, is of small consequence when, at the present time, it is not economically feasible to extract this valuable metal from the sea.

Although the sea contains a large amount of sulphur no attempt has yet been made to extract pure sulphur from sea-water on a commercial basis. Sources of sulphur in the Earth's crustal rocks are well able to meet the needs of present industry. Sulphur compounds, especially magnesium sulphate, or glauber salts, are, however, extracted from sea-water by evaporation processes.

The metal magnesium is extracted from sea-water on a large commercial scale. Magnesium is the lightest of the industrial structural metals, being only a little more than half as heavy as aluminium. It is particularly useful for the manufacture of aircraft, spacecraft and other products for which light weight is an advantage. An important plant in Freeport, Texas, utilises the waters of the Gulf of Mexico for magnesium extraction. Freeport is the most important centre in the world for the extraction of metals from sea-water and a big proportion of the United States' magnesium requirements comes from the Freeport plant. At the plant, which operates in a way similar to that of an important magnesium plant at Hartlepool near the Tees estuary, sea-water is pumped into a settling tank where it is mixed with calcium carbonate. The calcium of the additive is exchanged with the magnesium of the sea-water which precipitates as insoluble magnesium hydroxide. This settles on to the bottom of the tank from which it is collected. Magnesium is then extracted from this precipitate by chemical and electrolytic processes.

The non-metallic element bromine is almost a monopoly of the ocean which contains some 99 per cent of the total bromine of the

Earth. Large plants have been established, especially in the Gulf of Mexico, for extracting bromine from the sea. Extraction plants at Freeport, Texas, provide the bulk of the United States' requirements of bromine. This element is used in the petroleum industry as an anti-knock agent in petrol. It is interesting to note that Tyrian Purple, the dye which figured prominently in the early Phoenician trading activities in the Mediterranean is obtained from the marine gasteropod-Murex, an animal which is extremely efficient in extracting bromine from the sea.

The element iodine is difficult to detect in sea-water, yet it is extracted in relatively large quantities at a relatively fast rate by most marine plants and by some marine animals as well. Iodine is obtained from sea-weed and is used widely in medicinal preparations.

One of the great advantages of the ocean as a storehouse of metals is that in the sea dissolved metals are uniformly distributed and they are available to any nation who wishes to exploit them. The distribution of mineral ores in continental rocks is by no means uniform. Economic and political factors influence greatly the exploitation and marketing of continental ores; and, in time of war, a nation may find herself cut off from her supplies. For strategic reasons, therefore, the exploitation of the minerals of the sea is of great importance.

As a result of the erosive effect of sea-waves on shores and cliff faces, and the discharge of suspended matter into the sea by rivers and streams, large quantities of beach material are to be found on sho ts and in the off-shore region. Beaches are interesting deposits from the point of view of mineral content.

Beach material is continually being fragmented and worn by the action of sea-waves and swell which meet the shore. Offshore currents, coupled with the swash and backwash of breakers and surf, are instrumental in sorting beach material. In general the finer material of beach is carried seawards and deposited offshore.

The bulk of beach-sand is made up of grains of quartz. Quartz sand, gravels and shingle, may be of considerable local importance for use in the building industry, especially sand for making plaster and gravels for concrete making. Quartz sand is also an important raw material in the glass-making industry.

Sand and gravel are dredged from the sea-bed in large quantities off the coasts of North-west Europe and eastern United States of America. As coastal urban areas expand they often cover, and therefore prevent exploitation of, the very building materials by which their expansions are sustained. In these circumstances seabed resources of sand and gravel acquire considerable commercial importance.

Minerals whose relative densities are greater than about 3·0 are classed as heavy minerals. These, if they occur in beach material, are often concentrated by the action of waves and offshore currents, as well as by wind which may blow the lighter fragments of beach away from the shore, into zones, or so-called stringers, within the beach. Stringers are usually found in backshore regions.

Submerged beaches in present-day offshore regions are sometimes rich in heavy minerals. Perhaps the most notable examples of submerged beaches from which valuable heavy minerals are extracted, are those of the submerged beaches of South-west Africa which contain diamondiferous gravels. Diamonds are being found in the gravels of these submerged beaches as deep as 100 feet and more. The South African Government granted concessions in 1961 to a company who has since exploited the marine diamonds in a region to the north of the mouth of the Orange River. The gravels are removed from the sea-floor by means of an airlift hydraulic dredger, and the production rate in 1962 averaged about 700 carats of gem-quality diamonds per day.

At the present time the most valuable mineral supplies obtained from a marine environment are those extracted from the rocks of the continental shelf. Of these minerals petroleum and sulphur are the most important. Large quantities of natural petroleum gas are also obtained from the bed of the sea. In tapping these resources the industrial corporations concerned have had to face and solve technical problems of great magnitude.

In the Atlantic region the continental shelf off Texas and Louisiana in the Gulf of Mexico, and the floor of the North Sea have been explored and geologically surveyed intensively, and offshore drillings are becoming more and more familiar in these areas. The sea-floor of the well-known Venezuelan Lake Maracaibo has been tapped for its valuable petroleum deposits for many decades, and the numerous oil-rigs which stand out of the lake bear witness to the immense amount of activity in this direction.

Underwater drilling for oil began in the Gulf of Mexico off the Texas coast in the 1930s. In the earlier years rigs were mounted on platforms built on piles driven into the sea-bed. If a well proved dry, as was often the case in the absence of modern geological prospecting techniques, the rig was usually abandoned at very great financial loss. To prevent such losses the submersible rig was developed. In this type of drill-rig, which was introduced in 1949, a pontoon forming the base for the columns which support the platform and drilling-gear rests on the sea-bed. These rigs have the advantage of being mobile, so that they may be towed from place to place. Their use, however, is limited to drilling in depths of water of not more than 150 feet.

An alternative arrangement to the submersible rig is the jack-up drill-rig, which was developed in the late 1950s. In this type of rig the self-elevating platform is supported by three or four legs which stand on the sea-bed; so that, like the earlier submersible rig, it could not be used for depths of greater than about 150 feet.

For drilling in deep water, floating rigs are used. These have the advantage of mobility and large capacity, but in high winds and rough seas drilling operations are seriously hampered on account of the lack of stability of the drilling platform. To meet the principal disadvantage of the floating rig the semi-submersible drill-rig has been developed. The platform of this type of drill-rig is supported on huge cylindrical columns carried on buoyancy chambers. These buoyancy chambers are suitably ballasted so that they are submerged to a sufficiently great depth at which wave influence is largely eliminated, thus providing great stability for the working platform.

Floating drill-rigs are moored in position by a suitable arrangement of anchors and chain cables provided that the depth of water is not too great. For drilling in very deep water, where the depth exceeds about 1000 feet, conventional mooring systems are impracticable. In the Mohole project, in which an attempt was made to drill through the Earth's crustal rocks to a level at least as deep as the Moho discontinuity purely for scientific purposes, a floating rig fitted with a system of computer-controlled positioning propellers was used to keep the platform vertically over the drill.

Extensive natural gas-fields have been discovered in the bed of the North Sea, and the nations of North-west Europe are at present busily engaged in exploiting these valuable deposits.

The mineral element sulphur is widespread in its uses. So numerous are its applications in industry that the extent of a nation's sulphur consumption is often regarded as providing a sensitive barometer of the state of the nation's economy. One of the chemist's most useful and least expensive raw materials is sulphuric acid. A great deal of this is used in the manufacture of artificial fertilisers and in petroleum refining. Sulphur is also used extensively in making drugs and in the vulcanising of rubber.

Commercial sources of sulphur in Sicily, which in earlier times were the most important deposits in the world, came under the control of a French company early in the 19th century, soon after an economic process of manufacturing sulphuric acid had been invented when a phenomenal demand for sulphur was created. The sulphur-producing industry was almost monopolised by the French, and this action spurred other industrial nations to develop their own sulphur industries. The English discovered a method whereby sulphur could be extracted relatively easily from iron pyrites. Later, in the 1890s, the German-born Herman Frasch discovered a unique method of extracting sulphur from the salt-domes of the Mexican Gulf coastlands.

A salt-dome is a curious geological feature consisting of an immense pillar of salt thrusting upwards from an ancient sedimentary salt-bed which is buried deeply in the Earth's crust. A salt-dome is sometimes capped with a sulphur-bearing limestone roof. Most salt-domes are barren of sulphur, only some 10 per cent of the salt-domes of the Gulf of Mexico region of Texas, Louisana and Mississippi, being productive.

Frasch based his method of extraction on sulphur's low melting-point. First a hole is bored from the surface to the bottom of the salt-dome cap rock. In this hole are placed three concentric pipes within a protective casing. The lower part of the largest diameter pipe is perforated. Hot water is forced between the two outermost pipes and this, on reaching the sulphur-bearing rock, liquifies the sulphur which is forced upwards through the middle pipe by water pressure within the rock, assisted by air which is forced downwards through the innermost and smallest pipe. The air serves to aerate and lighten the liquid sulphur so enabling it to reach the surface. One well is able to tap the sulphur from only about half an acre of dome cap-rock, so that new wells must be drilled frequently and new pipe-lines laid to bring hot water and air to the well and to take away the sulphur to storage tanks.

The largest sulphur producer in the world is the Freeport Sulphur Company which is operated from New Orleans in Louisiana. Freeport's Grand Isle sulphur mine is located seven miles from the coast of Louisiana. In the shape of a large letter Y the platform sprawls across the Gulf of Mexico for about a mile where the depth of water is about 75 feet. It is an artificial steel island reputed to be the largest of its kind in the world. At the base of the Y is an immense power-plant which supplies the hot water which is injected into the mine. Next to this are living-quarters and offices and a heliport. The two production platforms are located half a mile away, one at each end of the branches of the Y. The sulphur is pumped through a water-heated pipe-line which is laid across the sea-bed between the mine and the storage tanks ashore on the mainland seven miles from the mine.

The development of the vast undertaking of Grand Isle for sulphur extraction, and the sophisticated drill-rigs designed for extracting petroleum and natural gas from the rocks of the continental shelf illustrate the increasing complexity and costliness of modern mining techniques. But whatever the problems and whatever the cost, it appears that industry must be fed with sulphur and petroleum—these being two of the vital raw materials upon which the present-day industrial world depends.

A metal which is of considerable importance in the steel industry is manganese. This metal is used in the process of steel-making and also as an important steel alloy metal. With recent intensive local investigations of the abyssal floor, using undersea photography and other techniques, has come the discovery that there is on the sea-bed a widespread distribution of manganese in grains and nodules, as well as in the form of a coating on exposed rocks and as a replacement material of coral and other organic debris with which coral limestone rock is sometimes impregnated. This metal resource is as yet not being exploited, primarily on account of the difficulty of dredging it from the deep sea-bed on a sufficiently large scale to make it economically worthwhile.

Manganese nodules appear to be widely distributed and estimations in the order of 30,000 tons per square mile have been made for areas in the North-east Pacific. Although usually found at depths of 2000 fathoms or so, an interesting area in which the nodules are abundant lies off the South-east coast of the United States at a depth of not more than about 200 fathoms. The nodules contain about 24 per cent by weight of manganese, but perhaps of greater importance from an economic viewpoint are the other metals, particularly nickel, copper and cobalt, which occur in relatively large proportions in the nodules.

No doubt, as dredging and other recovery techniques are improved, and when the economic demand for it is sufficiently pressing, manganese and similar resources of the ocean environment will provide the needs of industry. And so it probably will be for many, if not all, of the scarce metals which exist in abundance in the marine environment. The ocean is truly a veritable treasure-house which has the potential of providing industrial wealth for mankind on an ever-increasing scale.

CHAPTER 9

ATLANTIC TRADE

1. Introduction

The earliest settled communities of Europe and the Near East appear to have evolved some 7000 years ago in the lands of the eastern Mediterranean. It was here that geographical conditions of climate and the availability of goods, water and other resources, favoured the rise of the earliest civilisations.

The ancient civilisations of Egypt and Babylonia, centred respectively on the Nile and the Tigris-Euphrates valleys, were based almost entirely on agriculture. With the progress of civilised forms of society, trade and commerce were to play increasingly-important roles.

Commerce covers the exchange of goods and the arrangements necessary to effect the exchange. The need for commerce begins only when neighbouring peoples have surpluses of commodities suitable for mercantile traffic. Exchange of goods between peoples of widely separated places requires some form of transportation system. If this system is primitive, the volume of trade tends to be small and the goods which enter it to be relatively valuable. Commodities such as oriental spices, oils, drugs and costly metal utensils, figured prominently in the trading ventures of the Egyptians and Babylonians. As civilisation advanced, the caravan trains of the desert land routes became subordinate to fleets of ships which plied the Mediterranean sea-routes.

2. Phoenician Traders

To ancient geographers the central section of the Syrian sea-board was known as Phoenicia. The Semites who settled in this region developed—unusually for Semitic peoples—an attraction for the sea, and the Phoenicians became the greatest maritime traders of antiquity. From their bases on the coast of Syria manufactured goods from the East were shipped by sea to Cyprus and Rhodes and to distant mainland centres of commerce in the eastern, and later the western, Mediterranean. Metalware and glassware, as well as textiles and spices, were exchanged for raw materials such as timber, unwrought silver, copper and tin. The Phoenicians were the first to demonstrate convincingly that long-distance sea-trade is profitable. To conduct their trade with increased security Tyre and Sidon—the two principal Phoenician trading emporia—founded colonies at strategic places within, and indeed outside, the Mediterranean area.

It was the valuable trade with Tarshish which led to the colonisation of the western Mediterranean littoral, and the Tarshish ships engaged in a trade in silver and copper which contributed significantly to Phoenician wealth. From Gades, in South-west Spain, Phoenician ships ventured northwards along the Atlantic European coasts of Spain and France to bring tin from North-west Spain and from the fabulous Cassiterides—the Tin Islands off the British coast. The colonies in South-west Spain, and in Mauretania on the Atlantic coast of Africa, were established as far back as the 12th century B.C.

That type of trade control over neighbouring peoples which results from one trading partner becoming politically organised to a more advanced stage than the others, came about in the cradle of civilisation under the Assyrian Empire during the middle of the eighth century B.C. The successful conduct of international trade is essentially a peaceful process, and the attempt of the Assyrians to control trade by cruel conquest was utterly unsuccessful. The Phoenicians were successful traders largely because they were peace-loving people who commanded the respect of all with whom they came into commercial contact. Nevertheless during the Assyrian domination of Phoenicia during the eighth century B.C., and later domination by the Greeks, Phoenician trading activities in the eastern Mediterranean were severely curtailed.

The Phoenician merchants who operated from Tyre and Sidon appear to have conducted their commercial activities entirely on the basis of simple exchange. Their successors, the Greeks, were instrumental in spreading the use of money. They introduced and maintained a silver currency which was not allowed to depreciate, and in which their trading partners had complete confidence.

3. Carthage

After the Phoenicians had been ousted from the eastern Mediterranean, the Phoenician colonies, which had been planted beyond the range of Greek influence, continued to prosper. Of these overseas colonies the most influential was Carthage. The history of Carthage dates from 813 B.C. when the first Phoenician settlement was established here. Following the decay of Tyrian and Sidonian power the Phoenician overseas colonies turned to Carthage as their natural leader.

The Carthaginians founded an empire which extended westwards from Carthage along the North African coast to the Pillars of Hercules and beyond. It included that part of the Iberian Peninsula south of the Ebro valley and the principal islands of the western Mediterranean. This empire was based on sea trade, and the power of Carthage rendered the western Mediterranean basin an exclusive trading region for Carthaginians alone.

Some two and a half centuries after the foundation of Rome, during which period Rome's power in the Mediterranean steadily increased, she was to enter into conflict with Carthage, the greatest city in the world at the time. Slowly, but inexorably, the Carthaginians were to lose command of the sea. Profits from trading dwindled and ultimately, during the middle of the second century B.C., Carthaginian traders were swept from the sea by their Roman rivals; Carthage was sacked; and the long-standing Phoenician influence in maritime activities came to an inglorious end.

4. Rome

The geographical position of Rome—far to the west of the centres of the more ancient civilisations—resulted, after Rome's rise to power, in a rapid advance of the frontiers of civilisation. The power of Rome was to extend westwards to the Atlantic shores and northwards into Gaul and Britain, and to all the lands to the south and west of the Rhine and Danube valleys.

Although Roman domination led to the rise of a great land empire the sea was not entirely unfamiliar to the Romans. Without familiarity with the sea it would not have been possible for Rome to have dominated, as she did, the whole of the Mediterranean coastlands. However, Rome was not a Carthage, and in the earlier phases of her history she took little interest in commerce and trade. After the destruction of Carthage and Rome's assertion of supremacy over the Greeks, the possibility of commercial development was explored.

Antioch, on the northern Syrian coast, continued to be the focal-point of the caravan routes from the East, and the principal items of trade, which catered for the wealthy, were the traditional spices, oils, drugs and silken textiles. These goods were shipped from the eastern Mediterranean to Rome and other centres of trade. The important port of Alexandria exported not only luxury goods, which had reached Egypt from Arabia by way of the Red Sea, but also large quantities of wheat, most of which had been exacted as tribute, to supply the increasing population of Rome. The luxury goods which entered Rome by sea, apart from those which were exacted by tribute, were paid for not by Roman exports but by silver, the drain of which was cause for complaint by Pliny and others.

5. Byzantium

During the whole of the third century B.C., the declining Roman Empire faced the attacks of Barbarians all along the European Imperial frontier. The Latin-speaking western half of the Roman Empire was first to collapse. In A.D. 324 Constantine the Great, the first Christian Roman Emperor, founded a new permanent capital at Byzantium, later to be named Constantinople in honour of its founder. Constantinople became the principal emporium in the whole of the Mediterranean region. Her favourable geographical position resulted in this great city becoming the centre of commerce between Europe and Asia.

Unlike Carthage, Alexandria or Rome, Constantinople developed not only as a commercial centre but as a great manufacturing region renowned for the quality of its numerous products. Fine textiles and leather goods, engraved and enamelled metal-work of exquisite workmanship, porcelain and mosaics, were exchanged for corn, salt, fish, wool and other raw materials, essential for her growing population and her thriving industries.

The merchants of Constantinople had the advantage of a strong currency and practised the principles of banking and marine insurance, with the aim of facilitating maritime trade and commerce. From the time of the fall of Rome to that of the Crusades, for nigh on 1000 years, Constantinople was a powerful commercial centre dealing with an immense amount of entrepôt trade.

6. The Rise of Islam

Islam was to play a predominant role in the later history of Europe and of the Atlantic. Under the prophet Mohamet the whole of the extensive Arabian peninsula became united during the early decades of the seventh century. The Arabs were essentially men of the land unaccustomed to the ways of the sea, but soon after they came to control the eastern Mediterranean, the nursery of the ancient Phoenician seafarers, they developed a strong navy which was to assist in the conquest of the North African lands to the west of Egypt, and of almost the whole of the Iberian Peninsula. This great Arab Empire grew up in little more than a century. Effective control from Arabia, over such a vast dominion, soon became impossible and, by the middle of the ninth century the Arab Empire had been divided into four distinct units each under a separate Caliph. The Western Caliphate, embracing Iberia, remained powerful until the beginning of the 11th century. At that time the Christian States to the north began to assert themselves and to advance southwards towards the Mediterranean. Gradually Christianity spread from the north and by the end of the 15th century, Granada, the southernmost region of Spain, was to become Christianised.

Under Islam, the Arabs controlled a vast trading area which extended westwards from Central Asia to the Strait of Gibraltar. It must not be forgotten, however, that although the power of Rome had been destroyed there were still civilised communities in the lands which hitherto had been ruled from Rome, and that the demand for luxury goods continued throughout the period of Arab domination. These goods were conveyed by Arab traders from the Orient, and the European trade in spices, especially pepper—of importance and in constant demand during mediaeval times for flavouring food—brought considerable profit to Arab merchants.

7. The City-States of the Western Mediterranean

Apart from Iberia, Islam did not spread into Europe, and there grew up in favourable places trading centres which were to gain considerable power during the Middle Ages. The beginning of the 11th century saw the rise of the City-States of Venice, Genoa and Pisa. Special trading privileges were granted to Venetian and Genoese merchants in Constantinople, and these Italian City-States profited by the decline of Constantinople under the aegis of whom they had developed. Venice, in particular, provided an excellent harbour from which the commodities brought in from the Levantine region of the Mediterranean could be distributed with relative ease to Central Europe.

The Italian City-States gained immensely from the trade that resulted from the Crusades, and by the 14th century they had established strong trading links, via the Atlantic route, with the flourishing ports of the Low Countries. Valuable spices and other eastern products were brought to the ports of North-west Europe and return cargoes consisted chiefly of wool and hides. The expansion of trade promoted industrial activity in both the Italian City-States and in the commercial centres of North-west Europe. Trade and industry were facilitated by improved techniques in commerce such as accountancy, the organisation of credit systems, and banking.

8. The Hanseatic League

The principal commercial centres of North-west Europe had, since the 11th century, co-operated with each other in order to foster their common trading interests. Out of such co-operation the powerful Hanseatic League emerged. The Hanseatic League was a confederation of essentially German commercial cities and towns which entered, like an independent State, into treaties with foreign powers. The main purpose of the League was to procure favourable trading concessions from rulers of foreign countries for their members. From about the middle of the 13th century to the beginning of the decline of the Hanseatic League, it held almost a monopoly of trade between the lands of North-west Europe. During the 15th century certain nations of North-west Europe, particularly England and Holland, became aware of their national strength, and this awareness was to bring about the fall of the League.

The Hanseatic merchants were engaged primarily in exchanging the products of northern Europe, especially those of the Baltic countries, including furs, timber, salt-fish and flax, for finished goods, especially fine textiles in which the Italian craftsmen of Florence and other centres specialised. The chief Hansa cities were Lubeck on the Baltic and Hamburg and Bremen on the North Sea, as well as important so-called counters in the out-lying trading-posts including those at London at the Steelyard, and Bruges in the Low Countries.

The quantity of commodities which entered sea-borne trade during the Middle Ages was relatively small. Most centres of population were self-sufficient in respect of the necessities of life to such an extent that the goods which entered international trade were luxury commodities. During this period oriental products in demand in North-west Europe reached market through the agency of the Italian commercial centres of Venice and Genoa. To a growing extent these were paid for by fine woollen textiles woven mainly in the Low Countries, England supplying a great part of the raw wool for this flourishing industry. Woven woollens were the first European manufactured products to figure in international trade.

In the eyes of the wealthier people of North-west Europe the valuable commodities of commerce were spices and silken goods from the East. In the course of time these people developed the desire to reach the Indies, the lands which yielded riches in the form of pepper and other spices, direct. The way overland was barred, the Arabs ultimately controlling the trade between East and West at the Isthmus of Suez. Moreover, the significant conquest of the Ottoman

K

Turks in 1453, when Constantinople fell into their hands, threatened the closure of the route by which the oriental goods reached the Levant. Prolonged disturbance in the eastern Mediterranean gave reason enough for northern European merchants to seek an independent route to the rich Spice Islands of the Orient. This dream was not to be realised until the closing year of the 15th century when Vasco da Gama returned to Portugal, after a memorable voyage, with a small consignment of spices from India.

9. *The Portuguese Traders*

The Portuguese made good use of the Atlantic islands which they had discovered; here they produced sugar-cane and the grapes for fine wine. Prince Henry had encouraged the economic development of Madeira in particular and, before his death, sugar, as well as wine from the Malvoisie grape, which Henry had introduced from Cyprus, were being sent to Portugal in considerable quantities. The Guinea coastlands were also exploited commercially, and gold-dust, ivory and slaves, became important items of trade.

Vasco da Gama demonstrated that the Atlantic and Indian Oceans were one, and his epoch-making voyage was to bring about momentous changes in the way of life of the people of North-west Europe. Within a few years of da Gama's voyage the Portuguese had spread their power to the whole of the coastlands of continental India and were in complete control of the spice trade of the East Indian islands. From that time onwards the trade between Venice and the Levant rapidly declined. It is little wonder, in the circumstances, that Venetian and Genoese seamen sought employment with the Western powers of Portugal and Spain, and later with France and England.

10. *The Emergence of North-west European Atlantic Traders*

A few years before Vasco da Gama's voyage to Calicut, Columbus, the Genoese navigator in the service of Castile, sailed westwards to discover the route, not to the Spice Islands of the Indies as he thought, but to a New World for Spain.

The voyages of da Gama and Columbus were to bring about a revolution in sea commerce. Although Portugal and Spain set out to claim exclusive rights in the exploitation of trade on the newly-discovered routes, England was not without hope of discovering a northern passage to the East and in so doing establishing markets for her woollen goods in the cold northern lands along the hoped-for route.

Richard Chancellor, the Chief Pilot in Sir Hugh Willoughby's ill-fated voyage in which a North-east passage was sought discovered the White Sea.   Chancellor was instrumental in obtaining for the English trading concessions with the Russians.   On the basis of these concessions the English joint stock company, which became known as the Muscovy Company of Merchant Adventurers, was formed in 1555.   A lively trade between England and Russia was established in which English woollens and corn were exchanged for the furs and forest products of the far North.

The search for the North-west Passage was a persistent endeavour of the English from the time of the earliest attempts made by the Cabots, Frobisher, Davis and Baffin.   Nevertheless, English merchants continued to be interested in the traditional route leading to the products of the East, and in 1581 a company was formed, which was later incorporated as the Governors and Company of Merchants of the Levant, with the aim of trading direct with Turkey and the eastern Mediterranean.

The Portuguese were highly successful in their endeavours to profit from their discoveries.   They established control of the Indian Ocean trade by diverting to their own ships the goods which hitherto had been shipped in Arab craft.   The Spanish, on the other hand, seemed not to be interested in trade.   Uppermost in their minds was the possession of gold and silver and precious stones.   These valuable commodities were obtained by forced native—and later imported African slave-labour, and were used in the homeland to buy essential commodities from abroad and to finance the endless succession of wars in which Spain found herself.

Soon after the Portuguese commercial conquest of the Indian Ocean took place, a large consignment of Eastern spices—pepper, nutmeg, ginger and cloves—reached a Portuguese factory in the Low Countries.   This factory, at Antwerp, was to become the centre of distribution of oriental spices to North-west Europe.   The demand for these articles in North-west Europe during the 16th century seemed to have been insatiable, and the Portuguese flourished accordingly.   The India trade was a crown monopoly of Portugal, and this system was ultimately to bring disaster upon her.   The Crown financed the Indies voyages and sold the cargoes in Lisbon almost entirely to foreign merchants.   Lack of capital in the homeland resulted in the merchants being asked to lend money for the much-needed capital.   As creditors and middlemen, the foreigners, therefore, absorbed almost all the profit of the Portuguese Crown's ventures.

The Castilian trade with the West Indies was organised on the basis of a Spanish public monopoly under the control of the merchants of Seville. The cargoes from the early Spanish settlements in the West Indies and Central and South America consisted of sugar, hides and a little gold, in return for agricultural equipment and essential foodstuffs, such as olive oil and wine, which could not be produced by the settlers during the early days of the colonisation. As the colonies grew, and exports to the homeland increased in value, the demand in Spain for capital to meet the increased trade could not be met. As a result of this much of the wealth of the Spanish Indies trade fell into the laps of foreign merchants, mainly Genoese and North Europeans

The Spanish American colonies developed an economy based on agriculture, ranching and mining. For their sugar and other plantations, they required slave-labour, a requirement which created a lucrative trade in, and market for, African slaves.

During the middle of the 16th century the rich silver deposits of Peru were discovered. This led to a rapid increase in the Spanish population of South America, with a corresponding increase in the demand for an ever-widening variety of manufactured goods. By this time large quantities of silver, as well as hides and sugar, were exported to Spain. In addition such commodities as tobacco and other indigenous American products reached the markets of Europe.

Most of the bullion that found its way to Spain was shipped at one or other of the Atlantic ports of the Isthmus of Panama, having been brought thither by ship along the Pacific coast to the Isthmus and then by mule-train to the port of Nombre de Dios.

Besides the natural hazards of the sea, such as shipwreck through grounding or rough seas, the Spanish vessels faced the possibility of attack by pirates or privateers. In the early decades of the 16th century organised convoys of Spanish treasure-ships were instituted. The convoy system added greatly to the expense of transport and provided no certain guarantee of safety, as convoy stragglers often became prey to marauders and, in times of war, whole convoys were sometimes attacked and destroyed or captured.

Failure of Spanish merchants to supply the needs of the colonists led to foreigners—Portuguese, English, French and Dutch—entering into the Spanish trade.

Portugal had, in the early 16th century, gained a foothold in South America. Brazilian sugar became the principal item of commerce shipped from the Portuguese American possessions. The slave-trade during the early days of the European colonisation of America was in the hands of the Portuguese from whose West African territories most of the slaves came. Portuguese slavers were licensed by Spain to sail from Lisbon to New Spain, but many sailed unlicensed direct from the Guinea coast to supply the sugar growers of the Spanish Caribbean islands and the silver mines of South and Central America.

In 1562, Sir John Hawkins successfully broke into the Indies trade when his small fleet of three ships sailed from England to West Africa where some 300 slaves were procured. Hawkins sailed to Hispaniola where his human negro cargo was exchanged for one of sugar and hides, which he brought home to England, the voyage yielding a handsome profit. A subsequent voyage in 1557 in which Hawkins and his cousin Francis Drake took part ended in disaster, three of the five ships which formed the slaving fleet being sunk by the Spanish at San Juan de Ulua, the port which served the city of Mexico. There followed a long period of piracy and privateering in the Caribbean with Drake as the central figure. This culminated with open war between England and Spain. In 1604, when James I succeeded Elizabeth, a peace treaty between England and Spain paved the way for English exploitation of unoccupied parts of America.

In 1609 the Dutch emerged as an independent nation and in due course Holland was to become, for a time, the master of ocean trade. The wealth of Holland during the Middle Ages stemmed from her well-organised fisheries. The herring fishing of the North Sea which, during the Middle Ages was an almost complete monopoly of the seafaring Hollanders, provided a nursery for seamen and also a valuable commodity greatly in demand in Europe.

The Dutch, by breaking down the monopolies of the European trading nations, became the principal maritime carriers for the whole world. They entered into the West Indies and American smuggling trade shipping slaves from West Africa, and in the early 17th century they were actively engaged in trade with Hispaniola and Cuba. They exploited successfully the extensive salt deposits of Cumana in Venezuela, employing ships' crews to dig out the salt and to load it into their ships. An immense quantity of this raw material, valuable to the fish-salting industry of Holland, crossed the Atlantic to Europe when the traditional Portuguese supplies were not available to the Dutch.

As Dutch trading interests with America increased the commercial importance of the city of Amsterdam grew until she became the principal market in Europe for American commodities. The formation of the Dutch East India Company in 1602 also brought great wealth to Amsterdam which became the North European market for Eastern goods as well as for those from the Americas.

The Dutch West India Company was formed in 1621, and Piet Hein—the Francis Drake of Holland—became the most celebrated of the Company's captains. The West India Company aimed not only at commerce with, but also at conquest of, the Spanish American possessions. The small islands of Curaçao, Aruba, Saba and St. Eustatius were seized between 1630 and 1640, and these became important trading depots. The Dutch also occupied the lands in the vicinity of the mouth of the Hudson. The colonists of this settlement, known as New Amsterdam, had easy access to a rich hinterland of timber and other forest products, especially furs.

The Dutch who settled in New Amsterdam in 1624 were not the first Europeans to settle in North America. The earliest successful English settlement was established in 1607 on the eastern seaboard at Jamestown. The Pilgrim Colony at Plymouth was established in 1620, and the Massachusetts Bay Colony in 1630. The English colonies were, in time, to absorb the Dutch, as well as the French and Swedish American settlements which had established themselves in the New World. Soon after ocean traffic had been developed between Holland and America English merchants endeavoured to supply the home market with foreign commodities more cheaply than could the Dutch. The endeavours brought about friction between England and Holland. A substantial increase in the price of essential spices imposed on Britain by Dutch merchants was instrumental in the setting up of the English East India Company. This famous joint stock company received its charter in 1600. The first voyage of an East India ship took place in 1601 and the venture was a glowing success. From its small beginnings the East India Company was to find itself dealing, not only with the products of the East, but also with the revenues and territories of the Indian princes and ultimately with the destiny of the Indian sub-continent.

From the early 17th century British sea commerce continued to spread, and more and more the English came into conflict with the Dutch. In 1651, by Cromwell's Navigation Act, all imports into England and her overseas territories in America were to be carried in English ships or those of the country of the goods. This brought England and Holland into open conflict, and by 1674 the former had gained effective control of the sea-trade of all Western Europe.

During the 17th century an important commercial principle was recognised and acted upon by England. This principle stated that to increase her national wealth the value of a nation's imports must never exceed that of her exports. In other words, a favourable balance of trade is a *sine qua non* of a successful commercial nation. The trade with the Baltic countries and Russia at the time was recognised as being greatly out of balance. The importations of timber, for masts and spars, and turpentine and other important naval stores, far exceeded in value the English exports to these countries. The realisation of this and other similar trade anomalies stimulated attempts at producing those goods, which were much in demand in Britain, in the American colonies. It seemed that to England, and other European countries as well, possession of overseas colonies afforded a means of escape from the supposed disadvantages of unfavourable balances of trade.

During the 18th century the Massachusetts Bay Colony rapidly grew prosperous and Boston became the leading port of North America. The forests of the hinterland provided oak for ships' hulls and tall pines for masts and spars. It is little wonder, therefore, that this region became a great shipbuilding centre. At the end of the Colonial period of North America the shipyards of Salem and other New England centres were supplying England with no less than a third of her ships. New England merchants by this time had also discovered and exploited the African–West Indian Trade in slaves and sugar and rum.

The discovery, in 1612, of a method of curing tobacco revolutionised the economy of the English American colonies where tobacco could successfully be grown. The tobacco planters adapted themselves to a system of trade at a distance, and London and Bristol, and later Liverpool, became their principal markets.

The colonists of the Carolinas, making Charleston their chief port, exploited their valuable forest lands which were to become the source region of the finest supplies of naval stores.

England's American and West Indian colonies were producers of great quantities of tobacco, sugar and other important products. Up to the beginning of the 18th century it was English merchants who supplied the European markets of Holland and France. In a later period it was England's successful attempt to be the entrepôt for such goods as tobacco and sugar from the West Indies and America, and tea from the East, which prompted Napoleon to dub the English a nation of 'shopkeepers'.

The importance attached to trade in sugar, tobacco and tea, was an indication of the change which had come about in the nature of sea-trade. No longer did international commerce supply merely the luxury needs of the wealthy as had hitherto been the case, but from the 17th century onwards the commodities of commerce were essentially the necessities of everyone. These commodities, imported on an ever-increasing scale, were paid for by industrial goods manufactured in the importing countries. This paved the way for the

Industrial Revolution in Europe which began in Britain. Soon after, the British found themselves at the manufacturing centre of the world, as well as being shopkeeper to the world.

Raw cotton, mainly from the American colonies, came into Britain in large quantities to serve the expanding textile industry. Cotton textiles had become very important items of world trade during the 13th and 14th centuries, the bulk of this trade being handled by the Hansa merchants of Germany. The Portuguese built up with India an extensive trade in raw cotton soon after Vasco da Gama's voyage. It was the Dutch trade with Lisbon during this time which brought Antwerp, Bruges and Haarlem to their eminence as cotton-manufacturing centres during the 16th century.

Following the decline in the power of Spain during the late 16th century, and the setting up of the English, Dutch and French East India Companies, Indian calicoes figured prominently in the direct sea-trade between North-west Europe and India.

Religious strife on the continent of Europe during the 17th century played a big part in Britain's rise to industrial might. Many thousands of Protestant textile artisans migrated to England where a domestic cotton-manufacturing industry rapidly grew. By the end of the 17th century Britain had established herself as the world's leading cotton textile manufacturer.

Cotton growing had been introduced in the new English-American colonies of Virginia and the Carolinas, and also into the West Indian islands. The cotton grown in the mainland American colonies during the early days was produced almost entirely for colonial use, but that grown in the West Indian islands was exported to Britain. By the 18th century about three-quarters of Britain's raw cotton requirements came from the West Indies. The invention of the cotton gin in the late 18th century gave an impetus to American cotton production, and by the beginning of the 19th century the United States' exports of cotton to England were substantial. The first successful United States' cotton-mill was set up in Rhode Island in 1790, but the primary source of cotton goods continued, until the wars of the present century, to be in Lancashire.

The great port of Liverpool owed its rise to the South Lancashire cotton industry. By the beginning of the 19th century competition with Liverpool was to spell decline for the port of Bristol, which hitherto had been Britain's second port. Bristol's prosperity, during the 18th century, had been based on African slaving, a lucrative trade in which Liverpool merchants also engaged. With the abolition of slaving in Britain in the mid-19th century the West Indies sugar industry suffered. This, in turn, led to a diminution in the commercial activities of Bristol. The establishment of a regular Atlantic slave-trade paved the way for a triangular route, a system which ship-owners endeavoured to establish in order to avoid a return voyage without cargo. The earliest triangular route for English vessels, a route which persisted for about two centuries, was a run from England to West Africa with trinkets to exchange for slaves; then across the Atlantic to the West Indies where slaves were exchanged for sugar and rum; and then back to England westwards across the Atlantic.

11. The American Independence

American shipowners, during the early days of independence, developed a big trade with China. It was the eastern trade, the monopoly of which was lost to the English East India Company in 1814, that attracted the New Englanders. General cargo was shipped to the East via the Cape route and tea was the principal commodity from China. In colonial days American shipping was hindered by restrictive English legislation, but soon after independence was declared, a lucrative trade between the New England States and the West Indian Islands was established.

The direct route across the North Atlantic between Europe and North America was comparatively neglected until the beginning of the 19th century when the famous Western Ocean Packets, financed by enterprising American merchants, ranked as the finest and fastest sailing-ships of the day. These craft catered for the large numbers of migrants from the countries of North-west Europe who entered the newly-formed independent United States of America.

12. The Age of Steamships and Motor-ships

With the advent of steam for marine propulsion, the route from Europe to the Far East via the Cape of Good Hope by steamship was attempted. This was found to be too expensive, and an alterna-tive arrangement was sought. This was to involve a sea-route from Europe to Alexandria in Egypt at which port goods were unloaded and passengers disembarked to travel overland to Suez on the Red Sea. Here steamers loaded for the final stage of the voyage. The expense of transhipping cargo at Alexandria and Suez, and the inconvenience to passengers on this route, favoured the sailing-ship passage to the East via the Cape. Until the Suez canal was opened in 1869, the famous English Blackwall frigates handled most of the traffic between Europe and the East. The Suez Canal, however, was to spell doom to the Cape route, especially for the clipper-ships of the first half of the 19th century.

During the final decades of the 19th century the Cape Horn route between Europe and the Far East became an important steamship route. By this time the trade between Britain and her Australian and New Zealand possessions had become prosperous. Sailing-vessels, however, continued to be prominent as wool and grain-carriers well into the 20th century. Many of the sailing-vessels on the Australian run were engaged on a triangular route from Europe to Australia by way of the Cape of Good Hope with European-manufactured goods. On discharge, Australian coal from New South Wales was loaded for the West-coast ports of South America. From these ports nitrates and phosphates were loaded for home, the Cape Horn route being used for the final stage of the voyage.

The applications of steam-power to industrial manufacturing and transport enlarged enormously the scope of commerce. Railways opened up continents and steamships speeded up voyages. Great Britain, in her multiple role as the manufacturing centre of the world, the ruler of the seas, and the supplier of the world's capital, prospered during the two centuries between 1700 and 1900 as no other nation had prospered before.

To facilitate the selling of her manufactured goods to the world the policy of Great Britain during the 19th century was to open her ports to receive freely raw materials from all countries. The swing from an essentially agricultural to a highly industrial nation, coupled with a prodigious rise in population, necessitated the importation of large quantities of grain and meat for which hitherto Britain had been self-sufficient. Britain's financial resources were placed at the disposal of overseas countries, especially those of South America, for the building of vast railway systems and other projects designed to increase the production of those raw materials, especially food, which had commercial value.

The opening up of the prairie lands of Canada and the rich grasslands of Argentina and Uruguay, largely by British capital, secured the guarantee of plentiful supplies of food for Britain. The merchant ships sailing under the Red Ensign were protected by a powerful British Navy having strategically-placed bases throughout the world. The so-called freedom of the seas in British eyes meant control of the seas, and the ships of the whole world, not only of Britain, sailed in perfect freedom during the long period of *Pax Britannica*.

Britain's plentiful supply of domestic coal, especially that of South Wales, was to feed the world's bunkering stations during the period from the advent of the steamship to the time of the Second World War. Most of these bunkering stations, located conveniently along the principal oceanic arteries of commerce, were owned by British interests. A great deal of coal was exported from Britain by trampships. A prominent triangular route in the hey-day of the British trampship during the early part of the present century, was coal to Italy or other Mediterranean country, thence in ballast to a Black Sea port at which grain was shipped for North-west Europe. In later years, following the rise of Communism in Russia, instead of Black Sea grain, British trampships brought home North African iron-ore or esparto grass. Coal to Argentina or Uruguay and grain— wheat, oats, barley or maize—for Europe was another common trampship run during the first four decades of the 20th century. Outward passage with coal or anthracite from Britain to Eastern Canada with grain for the homeward journey was yet another prominent trampship voyage.

The opening up of the Panama Canal in 1914 brought about significant changes in the pattern of Atlantic shipping-routes. The Cape Horn route declined in importance, the canal route providing a shorter and less expensive passage between Europe and the eastern North American ports with those of the Pacific coasts of North and South America.

Towards the end of the 19th century the process of industrial development made great strides in countries other than Great Britain. In particular the United States of America and Germany, both of whom possessed large resources of coal and iron-ore, became great manufacturing countries. Now an industrial nation is essentially urbanised and depends upon markets abroad for an outlet for its manufactures. As the industrial power of a nation develops she also becomes dependent on outsiders for the necessary raw materials to supplement her own domestic resources. A developing country, therefore, cannot afford to be independent of others. The industrial growth of many nations, which took place during the latter part of the 19th century, resulted in the emergence of a commercial system based on a curious blend of competition and interpendence. It is this system which, even today, results in rival industrial countries often being the best customers of each other. This follows because highly organised industrial countries offer the best markets for a wide range of finished, particularly luxury, products. A characteristic feature of trade at the present time, therefore, is the close network of trade-routes which connect the commercially competing nations of the world. This network is very prominent in the seas of North-west Europe; the trade between the United Kingdom and the countries of continental Europe, for example, is far in excess of that between the United Kingdom and any other trading region.

During times of national prosperity it is not unnatural that there should be a tendency for shipowning companies to be set up. In times of trade depression the tendency is for shipping companies to amalgamate. During the present century, even in times of prosperity, the practice of amalgamation of shipping companies into large groups has been common.

The advent of the petroleum industry has had remarkable effects on ocean trade. The oil-tanker has become the predominant ship of the ocean, and the motor-ship using diesel oil for fuel, and the use of fuel oil for ships' boilers, has all but rendered the coal-burning steamship obsolete. The important oil regions of the globe are located in North America, South America, especially Venezuela, and the Middle East countries of the Persian Gulf. The principal oil-tanker routes link these places with North-west Europe, where major oil-refineries in the Netherlands, Great Britain and other European countries are to be found.

Since the recent discovery of vast oil resources of petroleum on the Arctic shores of Alaska, considerable discussion has centred on the feasibility of conveying crude petroleum by tanker through the Arctic seas from Alaska to the eastern United States seaboard and to North-west Europe.

In 1969 the 115,000 deadweight tons tanker the *Manhattan*, specially equipped and fitted for the task, demonstrated the possibility and the practicability of using the North-west Passage for commercial purposes. On September 1st of that year the *Manhattan*, on voyage from Philadelphia to Prudhoe Bay in Alaska, crossed the Arctic Circle in Baffin Bay. Nineteen days later she anchored off Prudhoe Bay, having completed a passage which, doubtless, will have an important influence in answering questions related to the future development of Arctic resources of petroleum and other minerals.

The benefits that might accrue from using the North-west Passage include the substantial savings in costs over alternative methods of transporting petroleum to Atlantic markets. In addition, an open North-west Passage, now that the technology of shipbuilding for severe ice conditions is available, could mean an international trade-route that might have a profound influence on Arctic development and world-wide trade patterns. In this connection it is interesting to note that the distance between Europe and the Far East by way of the North-west Passage is only a little more than half the normal distance by sea if the Suez Canal is by-passed or not available.

Not the least important effect of an open North-west Passage is related to the great resources of mineral ores which are located in the Canadian Arctic. This mineral wealth, including vast deposits of iron-ore in Baffin Island, tungsten, lead, copper, nickel and zinc, can become economically important only if easy access is established.

13. *Air Transport*

The ocean remains the principal highway of commerce and the major seaports of the globe are the great centres of industry and population. The air, however, is becoming increasingly important in respect of the transport of certain forms of goods. For Atlantic passenger traffic aircraft now handle the major part of this trade. For holiday tourist traffic by sea, however, luxury passenger ships apparently will always find a place.

The first notable event in the history of air transport occurred in 1900 when the first German *Zeppelin* was launched. This device was regarded by many as being capable of transporting heavy loads over long distances. For a time, until the Second World War, German lighter-than-air Zeppelins operated a lively service between the major European cities and, from 1932, a regular trans-Atlantic schedule for the *Graf Zeppelin* was in operation.

The Wright Brothers made history in 1903 when the first aeroplane flight was made. The first notable aeroplane flight over the sea was that made in 1909 when Bleriot flew across the English Channel.

The Atlantic Ocean was crossed by aeroplane for the first time in 1919, and within the following two decades to the eve of the Second World War, the North and South Atlantic were serviced by a complex network of air routes.

PART II

CHAPTER 10

THE POLITICAL AND STRATEGIC BACKGROUND

1. Introduction

The sea was described by the famous Lord Curzon as the most uncompromising, the least alterable, and the most effective of all natural frontiers. Certain it is that the waters of the ocean provide the most prominent break in the continuity of human population and the most significant barrier to human mobility.

For long ages in human history the Atlantic Ocean was an impassable barrier to human intercourse, but since the Age of Discovery it has been an open road—at least in times of peace—between the nations of the whole world. The great concentrations of population on the globe are all accessible to the ocean, and so important are the sea connections between them that, in a politico-economic sense, the concept of 'one ocean' is apt and valid.

The history of European colonisation began in ancient times following the development of sea transport in the waters of the Eastern Mediterranean. The early development, as we have seen in Chapter 9, was in the hands of the successful sea traders of Phoenicia. Phoenician merchants, finding it necessary because of trade expansion, planted colonies at suitably located places within the Mediterranean area, and thereby became the first colonisers.

The Ancient Greeks also established colonies on the Mediterranean seaboards away from their homeland. Some of these, like those of the Phoenicians, were set up as trading outposts; but most, which were quite independent of the parent State, were established for reasons other than trade. Population pressure, political discontent, as well as desire for adventure, all played parts in the colonising activities of the Ancient Greeks.

The Romans, in turn, were also great colonisers, but their reasons for planting colonies were different from those of the Phoenicians or the Greeks. The Roman colonies were essentially centres from which Roman influence in culture and civilisation could spread.

In the circumstances which prevailed during the centuries immediately after the collapse of *Pax Romana*, when organised mobility temporarily came to an end, law and order was possible only within reach of local magnates. Following the fall of Rome the whole of Europe entered a period of feudalism—a political system characterised by intense fragmentation of land into petty principalities, and an absence of communications between peoples of even adjacent territories. The feudal system reached Britain when William the Norman defeated the English king Harold in 1066 after which England was brought into intimate relationship with France and her political organisation.

The enlightenment which followed the European Dark Ages came with the re-establishment of efficient communications. After the fall of Rome, and before the advent of the Age of Discoveries which followed on the heels of the Dark Ages, the chief exponents of colonisation were the City-States of the Italian seaboard. The colonies of the powerful sea-trading centres of Venice and Genoa were trade-inspired and were similar in character to those of the Phoenicians of an earlier age.

2. The Opening-up of the Atlantic

Following the rise of the Italian City-States, which prospered during the later part of the Dark Ages, the centre of gravity of maritime trade shifted westwards to the Atlantic seaboard of Europe. The early voyages of exploration and discovery made by the adventurous Portuguese seamen sponsored by Prince Henry the Navigator, ushered in an era during which the Atlantic Ocean was to be transformed from a frightening and unknown watery wilderness into a vast arena of enterprising commercial and military activity. Henceforth the history of colonisation came to imply the spread of European influence to the remainder of the habitable world. The Age of Discoveries witnessed the slow opening of hitherto unknown lands which provided a vast new range of commercial possibilities and an increased scope of mass movements of people who were to emigrate from Europe to fill the newly-discovered territories overseas.

The greatest barrier to circulation, the ocean, was broken down by the discoveries of the 15th century. From that time onwards States which had grown up in maritime locations were not slow to realise the great advantage to be gained by securing, and indeed, expanding their territories by developing what came to be known as sea-power.

At the dawn of the Age of Discoveries the States of Western Europe, whose shores are washed by the waters of the Atlantic, included Portugal, Spain, France, the Netherlands, Germany, England, Denmark and Norway. Until the discovery of the ocean these States lay on the outer fringe of the world and their importance in world affairs was negligible. The Age of Discoveries was to change all this and the States of Western Europe were to dominate the world political scene for about half a millenium.

At first sight it would appear that the people of any one of the maritime States of Western Europe might have discovered the Atlantic Ocean. In a sense the Norsemen discovered it in the 10th century. These people were adventurous and fearless seamen, yet their discovery of Iceland, Greenland and North America, had little effect on the course of history. This is not to be wondered at: the lands discovered by the Norsemen were cold and barren and they failed to inspire the spirit of colonisation. The real discovery of the Atlantic Ocean was to be left to the Portuguese.

Portugual had expelled the infidel Moors from her territories; and the Portuguese, being accustomed to fighting for their Christian faith against Islam, continued to fight the Moors in North Africa. By the middle of the 15th century a Portuguese province had been established on the Atlantic coastland of the African continent, and the time had come for the discovery of the Atlantic.

3. The Portuguese and Spanish Atlantic Strategy

Prince Henry of Portugal hastened the course of events which led to the discovery of the new lands across the sea. He, more than any other man, paved the way for a new and exciting era in human history. By providing the facilities and giving inspiration and encouragement where necessary, he was instrumental in making sea exploration successful. In 1447 it was loudly and publicly declared for the whole world to know, that the Portuguese object of exploration and discovery was essentially to spread Christianity to the unfortunate heathens of the Guinea lands. Accordingly a grant was made to Portugal by the Pope—whose authority on these matters seemed at the time to be generally acceptable—of all lands then, or at any future time to be, discovered southwards of the African Cape Non. The papal grant of a monopoly to the lands discovered by the Portuguese was certainly not likely to be questioned by Portugal's rival, the Catholic Castile.

Soon after the initial explorations of the Guinea coastlands, Portugal became interested in the discovery of an Atlantic route to the Indies. Her energies were devoted to this end to an extent that she gave little or no interest to the idea that perhaps a way to the Indies lay westwards across the Atlantic. It was the Genoese navigator Christopher Columbus who endeavoured to interest the crown of Portugal in this possibility: and it was Castile, not Portugal, who ultimately was to sponsor the first attempt during the Age of Discoveries to seek a passage to the rich treasures of the East by sailing westwards across the Atlantic.

Following Columbus's voyage of discovery of the West Indies, the Spanish monarchs Ferdinand and Isabella sought papal support for a monopoly of trade and settlement in the newly-discovered lands. The Pope at the time, Alexander VI, was a Spaniard, and support for the crown of Spain, therefore, was readily forthcoming. Four Papal Bulls were issued: the first two—the second merely extending the privileges awarded in the first—granted to the Sovereign of Spain all lands discovered, or to be discovered, in the regions explored by Columbus. The third, which became known as the *Inter Caetera*, provided for a Spanish sphere of exploration to the west of a meridian lying 100 leagues to the west of the Azores and Cape Verde Islands. The fourth bull extended the previous grants to include all islands and mainland found, or to be found, in sailing towards the west or south towards India.

The fourth of these Papal Bulls gave alarm to Portugal who, at the time, was intent upon discovering a route to India by way of the southern Cape of Africa. The Portuguese king thereupon applied to the Pope in an endeavour, which in the event proved unsuccessful, to have the privileges of the bull limited. In 1494 the famous Treaty of Tordesillas was concluded between Portugal and Spain. By this treaty, which was a political triumph for Portugal, Portugal gained a legal claim to all lands which might be discovered east of a meridian extending from pole to pole and located 370 leagues west of Cape Verde. Spain was to have a legal claim to lands to the west of this line. It is interesting to note that neither the third Papal Bull, which formed the basis of the Treaty of Tordesillas, nor the treaty itself could possibly be applied, for at the time no certain way had been evolved for finding longitude at sea. However, on the basis of the Tordesillas Treaty Portugal was to lay claim to Brazil.

The discovery of the West Indies by Columbus was closely followed by exploration of the coastlands of the Caribbean Sea and the Gulf of Mexico. The conquest of Venezuela was completed in 1500, and that of Mexico, by Cortez, in 1524. Spanish colonists had settled in Paraguay and Colombia in the early decades of the 16th century, and the River Plate settlement at Buenos Aires was founded in 1535. The Mississippi was discovered in 1539, and at about the same time a Spanish colony was planted in Florida. Before 1540

L

Chile, Ecuador, Peru and Bolivia, had been added to the overseas possessions of the Spanish Crown. All these territories came under the direct rule of the Spanish sovereign, and the natives, as well as the colonists, were his subjects. In the space of comparatively few years Spain built up a great land empire in South and Central America.

The Brazilian coastlands of South America lay on the Portuguese side of the Tordesillas boundary line—which became known as the Pope's Line—and these came legally to be colonised by Portugal. The new colony—Brazil—received its name on account of its abundant supplies of brazil wood from which a commercially valuable red dye was obtained. Portuguese colonists gave the country its language and basic racial type. The first Portuguese explorers found a widely-scattered native population; and lack of European women led to the creation of large numbers of cross-bred European-Indians or Mestizos. Later the introduction of African negro slaves gave rise to a strong mulatto element in Brazil's population.

As far back as 1549 the Portuguese, fearing Spanish encroachments on their South American territory, pursued an active policy of settlement in Brazil. In contrast to the Spanish colonists in New Spain, who set out to conquer cities rather than to cultivate the land, Portuguese society in Brazil was essentially agricultural and rural in character. West African slaves served to supplement the native Indian population in the production of cane sugar for which Brazil was to become very important. Brazil reached the zenith of her colonial prosperity at the time when the rest of the Portuguese Empire suffered a decline under the rule from Spain.

4. Dutch Sea-power

In 1578, under the famous Prince of Orange, William the Silent, the Dutch had thrown off all effective control by Spain. Three years later, in 1581, King Philip II annexed Portugal as heir to King Henry, and for the following 60 years, a period known to the Portuguese as 'The Sixty Years' Captivity', Portugal was ruled by a Spanish sovereign.

After his conquest of Portugal the Catholic King Philip of Spain sought not only to re-establish the Pope's religion in the countries of North-west Europe, but also to establish his own personal supremacy in these countries. The disaster of the Spanish Armada in 1588 ruined Philip's plans and, moreover, the nations he had threatened—English, French and Dutch—allied themselves against Spain.

At enmity with Spain, and not recognising the edicts of Rome, the Dutch gradually acquired command of the sea. They soon established themselves in the Indian Ocean and captured the lucrative African-slave trade from the Portuguese. Before the end of the 16th century Dutch traders were to be found in the West Indies. Between 1630 and 1640 the Dutch seized the islands of Curaçao, Aruba and Bonaire, which lie off the Venezuelan coast: and the Antillean islands of Saba, St. Eustatius and part of San Martin. For the two decades between 1630 and 1650 the Dutch established themselves in Brazil after having successfully waged war on the Portuguese colonists, and were in control of slaving-stations on the West African coast.

The powerful Dutch West India Company was established soon after the opening of the 17th century, and organised fleets of the Company's ships operated in American waters. As well as these regulated operations, numerous private Dutch trading vessels were engaged in commercial operations and enterprises in the Atlantic: and, for a long period, the Dutch were the principal ocean traders among all maritime nations. In particular, Dutch shipping was to assist in the establishment and the consolidation of English and French colonies not only on the North American mainland, but also on those West Indian islands which had not been colonised by the Spanish. Not only did Dutch service help the new colonies, but it also angered Spain and hampered her progress.

Friction between Holland and England became intense in 1651 when Cromwell's Navigation Act of that year required that all imports into England and her colonies were to be conveyed in English ships or those of the country of the goods. This was a direct challenge to the Dutch and war between England and Holland inevitably followed. The contest between these seafaring nations for supremacy of the sea lasted for six decades.

War was first declared between England and Holland in 1652, and English soldiers and England's mercenaries were soon to fight Dutchmen on Dutch soil. Holland sought the aid of the French who, combined with the Dutch, fought England during 1666–7. By this time France herself had made a bid to become a great sea-power under Louis XIV, and during the war between them Holland and England saw that the French were profiting considerably by the former's loss of sea-trade. This led to a cessation of the war and the establishment of an uneasy peace which lasted until 1672.

In 1668 Louis XIV's attempt to succeed to the monarchy of Spain, in the name of his Spanish wife, met with failure. This led to a French attempt at invading the Netherlands. Holland checked this attempt but four years later in 1672, Louis, aided this time by England, invaded Holland. Britain withdrew from this war in 1674: and, being a neutral for the remaining part of the war, which lasted until 1678, she gradually gained and ultimately secured control of the ocean commerce which hitherto had been in the hands of the Dutch.

1688 is a significant date in European, as well as in English, history. This was the year of the revolution of the English Protestants against a Roman Catholic king who sought to impose his own religion on all his subjects. It was this revolution that transformed the English political system into a constitutional monarchy controlled by a powerful parliament.

The 1688 revolution brought England and Holland into a coalition. From that year, until 1713, England and her ally Holland were to ruin the maritime power of France, but during this period the maritime power of Holland was also eclipsed.

France's entry into America began with the exploratory voyage of Verrazzano, the Italian explorer who was engaged by the French king in 1524. This voyage was followed up by those of Jacques Cartier in 1534, 1535 and 1541. In his second voyage Cartier sailed up the St. Lawrence river as far as the site of present Montreal. The principal object of the 1541 expedition was colonisation. Several hundreds of men and women emigrated from France to form the new American colony of Charlebourg Royal. This experiment, like the first English attempt at settlement in the New World, was entirely unsuccessful. It was not until 1605 that the next French attempt at colonising in North America was made. This attempt was made by a Huguenot group who colonised Port Royal in Arcadia, later to become Nova Scotia. In 1608 the renowned explorer Champlain founded the French settlement of Quebec. The early French settlements were financed by a joint stock company—the Company of New France—which had been incorporated by Richelieu, and which sought to recompense the shareholders from profits made from fur-trading.

5. English Sea-power

The English took steps to resist the encroachment of the French in North America and, as early as 1613, clashes between English and French colonists occurred. Although there was organised warfare between English and French settlers whenever England and France were in conflict in Europe, this was not to displace the French from North America.

During the early decades of the 17th century, Dutch, French and English had gained footholds in Spanish America, where the three Guianas — Dutch, French and English — were ultimately established.

The Guiana coastlands were entirely unsuitable climatically for European settlers and the early attempts at colonisation failed. These failures were to have important indirect results in that, in many cases, unsuccessful colonists came to settle in those rich islands of the Lesser Antilles which had been ignored or neglected by the Spanish.

The important English settlement at Barbados was established in 1624, and Barbados and other English colonial West Indian islands became valuable suppliers of cane-sugar and cotton. The islands of Martinique and Guadeloupe, which were successfully colonised by the French, were in due course also geared to sugar and cotton production.

With the rise of Britain's sea-power at the beginning of the 18th century the organisation of international commerce fell into the hands of British merchants who had amassed great wealth largely through trading in maritime activities.

During the whole of the 18th century the supremacy of Britain's trade and her command of the sea were challenged again and again. From 1739 to 1763, with a break of eight years from 1748 to 1756, Britain was at war, mainly with France and Spain. These countries at the time of their wars with England were simultaneously at war with continental neighbours whom Britain supported from the profits of her sea trade. France's weakness at sea resulted, at the end of the Seven Years War with Britain, in French Canada becoming a British possession.

By the time of the Seven Years War, the English colonies in America had grown to acquire considerable economic strength, and their population had grown from about a quarter of a million in 1700 to about a million and a half.

The 18th century witnessed a new impetus to colonial expansion in America from the influx of European immigrants. Since the best land near the East coast had already been occupied, the newcomers were forced to push westwards beyond the coastal plain. By 1740 frontiersmen and their families had pushed over the Pennsylvania border into the valleys of the left-bank tributaries of the great Mississippi.

While the English were colonising the Atlantic coastal plain, the French had been planting a different type of dominion in the St. Lawrence valley. They had concentrated, in their colonising policy, on explorers and fur-traders rather than on agricultural settlers. They had pushed into the Great Lakes region and had taken possession of the Mississippi valley by establishing a line of forts and trading stations which marked out a crescent-shaped empire stretching from Quebec in the north-east to New Orleans at the mouth of the Mississippi in the south west. The French, therefore, were able to check the westward advance of the English colonists and in time the situation became critical. After eight years of conflict between French and English, the dream of a French empire in North America vanished. French Canada and the upper Mississippi valley passed into the hands of the English in 1762.

Britain was now to meet a new problem. The conquest of French Canada and her triumph throughout the colonial world in general—especially in India—brought Britain face to face with the problems of empire. Hitherto the British had formulated no consistent policy of empire for her North American colonies. These had been organised on the basis of a confirmed mercantilist principle whereby they were required to supply the mother-country with raw materials and to depend upon the mother-country for their manufactured requirements. Following the conquest of Canada the old colonial system had become inadequate for the requirements of the new situation, and England failed to keep American colonial matters under control. The ensuing revolution of English-American colonists against England elevated the American people to an independent place among the nations of the world. Peace negotiations between Britain and the Americans began in April, 1782, and were signed as final in the following year. The peace-treaty acknowledged the independence, freedom and sovereignty of the Thirteen States, to whom sovereignty to the unclaimed territory to the east of the Mississippi was granted.

The establishment of the United States of America raised a potential threat to Britain's dominance in the western North Atlantic; yet, more than a century was to pass before the United States developed into a contender for command of the Atlantic seas which wash her shores. The British Navy, from bases in Nova Scotia, Bermuda and the West Indies continued to exert influence on the sea-routes of the western Atlantic. In the eastern Atlantic Britain's position had been secure since 1704 when Gibraltar fell to the English. This gave Britain command of the entrance to the Mediterranean. Moreover, by blockading the narrow Gibraltar Strait Britain was able to divide the naval strengths of both France and Spain.

During the 19th century France was Britain's most dangerous rival for sea-power. The French, under the leadership of Napoleon, came within an ace of conquering the whole of Europe. Napoleon regarded India as being the source of Britain's commercial supremacy. He, accordingly, took steps to establish bases within the Mediterranean Sea and in the countries of the Middle East preparatory to an attempt to win India for the French. Britain's command of the sea thwarted French plans in this direction. An attempt was then made to cripple Britain's commercial relationships with the countries of northern Europe. Napoleon succeeded, in 1800, in rousing these countries to unite in an Armed Neutrality against Britain. Britain from then on was left to face France alone. The famous Battle of Copenhagen resulted in the destruction of the powerful Danish fleet and it was this British victory that led to the break-up of the Armed Neutrality. Napoleon then prepared plans to strike at the heart of Britain by invading her, but lack of French ships, and a powerful British Navy, doomed these plans to failure. In 1805 Nelson's destruction of the French fleet at Trafalgar effectively prevented a recurrence of the threat of a French invasion of the British Isles.

Napoleon set himself the task of subduing the whole of continental Europe in order to shut out Britain from continental markets. By skilful diplomacy, and brilliant military strategy where necessary, the French gained control of most of Europe. At this stage Britain declared that all continental trade must pass through British ports and that dues must be paid on all continental cargoes. This requirement was enforced by the ships of the Royal Navy which effectively controlled the British 'Narrow Seas'. Britain continued, therefore, to control the bulk of the sea commerce of Europe, and France consequently became progressively weaker and poorer. Coming ultimately into open conflict with Russia, the disastrous French expedition into that country in the winter of 1812, when Napoleon's forces were routed on the outskirts of Moscow, marked the beginning of the end of Napoleonic power in Europe. It also marked the beginning of a long era of *Pax Britannica*.

The Napoleonic Wars had a marked effect on the political relationships between each of the two principal contenders and the United States of America. The vast territory to the west of the Mississippi valley had long been held by Spain, but Napoleon had forced a weak Spanish Government to cede this great tract of land to France. When Louisiana, as this territory became known, came under French control, it appeared to many American politicians that a French plan was afoot for establishing a huge French colonial empire to the west of the Thirteen States. Napoleon, sensing the strong possibility of an alliance between England and the United States resolved to foster friendly relations with the latter. This he sought to achieve by inviting the United States to purchase Louisiana. Acceptance of this invitation would not only enrich Napoleon's treasury, but it would also put the territory out of the reach of Britain who, it seemed, was poised for a southward attack from her consolidated position in the Great Lakes region of Canada. In 1803, Napoleon's invitation was accepted and the Louisiana Purchase secured for France a large sum of money amounting to many millions of American dollars.

During the Napoleonic Wars the Americans, under their President Thomas Jefferson, had attempted to maintain neutrality. Both Britain and France, however, had set up blockades which had serious consequences for American seaborne trade. America, not unnaturally, was aggrieved; particularly at the British action of cutting off the rich American carrying-trade with the products of the French West Indies. A further grievance which aroused American feeling against Britain stemmed from the problem related to the immense Navy which Britain had built up, and the difficulty of keeping the ships of this powerful sea-force properly manned. Poor conditions of service in the ships of the British fighting fleet made it almost impossible to recruit men from home. Moreover, desertion to American ships was very common. In the circumstances Britain regarded it as a right to search American ships on the High Seas and to take off any British subjects on board. This action humiliated America, and the impressment of hundreds of bona fide American subjects angered the American Government and people. Ultimately, in 1812, the United States declared war on Britain. During the Anglo-American War, which was brought to an end in 1815, Britain successfully blockaded United States ports from British naval bases in the western Atlantic.

Following the decay of Spanish influence in Central and South America, the strong influence of the British was felt during the struggle for control of the Central American isthmus, and the Atlantic approaches to it. Britain possessed several strategically-placed islands within the Caribbean Sea and had coveted eyes on the Spanish island of Cuba. A British objective was to control the routes leading to a possible inter-oceanic canal which had been proposed for the isthmus. Had Britain been successful in strengthening her influence in this region she would have gained a leverage on the United States comparable with that which she held over Europe. James Monroe was foremost amongst American statesmen in recognising this danger, and in the famous Monroe Doctrine of 1823 the United States warned all European powers not to interfere with the newly-liberated Spanish colonies in the western hemisphere.

During the 16th century the Caribbean Sea and the Mexican Gulf came under the dominance of Spanish sea-power. Spain was paramount in this region in that she controlled the coastlands of Central America and also the large Caribbean islands of Cuba and Hispaniola. The numerous Caribbean islands, however, made it impossible for Spain to defend all of them, so that in the course of time she was forced to recognise the interests of England, Holland and France, in the islands of the West Indies, especially those of the Lesser Antilles.

During the 19th century the United States became increasingly interested in the seas of Central America. This surge of interest stemmed from the Louisiana Purchase of 1803; the acquisition of Florida in 1819; the annexation of Texas in 1845; and the setting up of the State of California in 1850.

The Latin American mainland States became independent political entities between 1804 and 1903. This hundred-year period began in the year when the negro republic of Haiti emerged, and ended when the republic of Panama, hitherto a part of Colombia, was established in 1903. Argentina declared her independence in 1810, and Brazil declared its independence from Portugal in 1822. In 1879 Uruguay, whose territory originally formed part of Brazil, was set up as a buffer State, largely through British intervention, between Portuguese-speaking Brazil to the north and Spanish-speaking Argentina to the south of the Plate estuary. In the northern part of Spanish South America, Venezuela and Colombia declared their independence from the Crown of Spain in 1811 and 1831 respectively.

Following the Spanish-American War of 1898 Cuba gained independence, leaving the island of Puerto Rico the last Spanish-speaking colony in the New World. In 1917 Puerto Rico was granted a constitution which conferred United States citizenship on its people.

With the rise of United States power in Central American waters the question of an isthmus canal became one of great strategic importance. America felt that her Navy must be able to operate in both Atlantic and Pacific in order adequately to protect her eastern and western shores. When Colombia hampered the demands of the United States to cut an isthmus canal, the Americans were instrumental in recognising the independence of the Panamanians of the southern and narrowest part of the Central American isthmus. In 1903 a treaty with the newly-formed State of Panama allowed for a perpetual lease of a strip of land, now called the Canal Zone, within which a canal was to be built. The Panama Canal was opened for commercial traffic during the second decade of the present century.

Since that time it has become of diminishing importance as a strategic focus, but it has grown in commercial importance as a crossroads of sea-routes operated by the United States for the benefit of all the world's maritime nations.

The rapid growth of the industrial might of the United States, following the American Civil War of 1861–65, was matched by United States naval expansion to such an extent that Britain was confronted with a dilemma. She found that she should either strengthen her naval bases in the western Atlantic or lose control of the waters of the Caribbean Sea and the Gulf of Mexico. This dilemma was resolved in favour of the United States largely because of the technological changes which took place during the second half of the 19th century.

During the first half of the 19th century no fundamental changes took place in the design of naval ships nor in their fighting equipment. Soon after mid-century, however, the transition from sail to steam, and from wood to iron and then steel, as well as the implementation of radical changes in ships' armaments, accelerated the obsolescence of Britain's naval fleets. This was to give Britain's rivals a chance to compete for sea-power on nearly-even terms. The second half of the 19th century witnessed a period of active naval expansion on a world scale. Not only did the United States give increased attention to sea-power, thereby thwarting Britain's attempt at gaining dominance in American waters, but several European States launched ambitious naval building programmes.

Italy rose to prominence in the Mediterranean at about the time of the opening of the Suez Canal in 1869. The occasion of the opening of this important artificial waterway marked a significant epoch in the history of maritime commerce. The new all-sea route between Europe and the Far East was superior in every way to the Cape route. With the opening of the canal came a political struggle for the control of the strategic places along the route. France and Italy, as well as Great Britain, were active in this respect. France had occupied Algeria during the period 1830–47, and ultimately Italy was to gain a foothold in Libya. Britain, however, possessed political control over Egypt from 1882 until 1936 during the whole of which time she occupied a military base in the Suez Canal zone.

The interests of European maritime powers in the Atlantic coastlands of the African continent were confined, until the closing decades of the 19th century, to calling-points such as Algoa Bay and Table Bay at which ships could store and water and carry out repairs if necessary; and to trading stations, particularly those connected with the slaving-trade of the Guinea coast. Towards the end of the

19th century conditions were ripe for the opening up of the Dark Continent, and the so-called European 'scramble for Africa' began. From then until our time, most of the African continent came under rule from European capitals.

6. The Twentieth Century

By the 1870s France, Russia, Italy and Germany were busily engaged in modernising their naval fleets. Germany's rapid military and industrial development, which followed in the wake of the unification of the German States under Bismarck, was cause enough for British anxiety. This anxiety, formerly directed to France and Russia, was now transferred, during the closing decades of the 19th century, to Germany.

In 1900 Germany launched a major naval programme which Britain feared might break Britain's control of the seas. From this time the United Kingdom, openly recognising the supremacy of the United States in the western Atlantic, set out to cultivate the good-will of America towards Britain. This policy was to bear fruit in the time to come. The United States consistently ranged herself on the side of Britain during the succession of crises, commencing with the Boer War of 1899–1902, which Britain faced during the military rise of Germany. The menace of Germany had the effect of suppressing the traditional rivalry between Britain and France.

Following the declaration of the European War of 1914 the naval resources of Russia and Japan were added to those of the Anglo-French combined fleets. Later the United States naval forces were added to these so that the Allies under the leadership of Britain, held effective command and control of the Atlantic. The German merchant marine was soon driven from the oceans and the blockade of Germany, which was ultimately to bring about her military defeat, commenced.

As the Great War progressed the German reply to the Allies' command of the sea was a large-scale submarine offensive which almost brought disaster to the Allies.

The Great War in Europe, which came to an end in 1918, saw the destruction of German sea-power, and Britain again held undisputed command of the eastern Atlantic and its peripheral seas. During the war the United States had developed into a major sea-power and, as a result of the Washington Conference for the limitation of armaments held in 1921–22, the Americans recognised Britain's strategic interest in the eastern Atlantic. The British, in turn, recognised the western Atlantic as falling under United States control.

The military rise of Germany and Italy under Hitler and Mussolini respectively, led to the outbreak of the second phase of the 20th-century World War. The military aeroplane and the aircraft-carrier, as well as the submarine, were to play important roles in the Battle of the Atlantic, in which the task of keeping open the shipping-lanes connecting Britain and North America was a life-or-death struggle for the Allied naval and air forces.

The industrial and military growth of Germany during the period 1920–39 undermined British security by endangering the sea-lanes which are the means of supplying Britain's industries with vital raw materials. It was clear, that during this anxious period for Britain, the British could not command the Atlantic alone. On the other hand, the United States, in not having strategic bases in the eastern Atlantic could not exercise control over the whole of the Atlantic single-handed. But Britain and the United States in partner-ship possessed the requisites for effective command of the Atlantic.

Following the cessation of the World War in the European theatre in 1945, the question as to the feasibility of the control of the seas arose. New weapons of destruction had become available and the concept of sea-power, which hitherto had been related to tradi-tional naval forces and techniques, changed radically with the introduction of these new devastating weapons.

The period immediately following the World War witnessed the remarkable advent of the U.S.S.R. as the dominant military power of Europe. The U.S.S.R. and the U.S.A. now stand as the two great military protagonists occupying the world's political arena.

In the present geo-political pattern the North Atlantic is to be regarded as providing defence in depth for the United States. Many of the countries of Europe, including Norway, Denmark, the Netherlands, Belgium, Portugal, Italy, Greece and Turkey, as well as Great Britain, have aligned themselves with the United States and Canada to form the North Atlantic Treaty Organisation (N.A.T.O.). This supra-national organisation forms the basis of the united defence of the capitalist nations should war break out between capitalism and communism—the two apparently irreconcilable social systems which dominate the present world politico-economic scene.

Since 1945 when the Cold War between East and West began, the strategic policy of the United States has been to establish a ring of bases which encircle the communist countries of Eurasia. The principal arc of this defence system comprises military bases in Alaska, northern Canada, Greenland, Iceland, Britain and other European countries in western and southern Europe.

7. Territorial Waters

In the international law of the sea the term Territorial Waters applies to the zone of sea adjacent to the coast of a littoral State over which the State exercises sovereignty subject to the rights of innocent passage belonging to foreign States. Outside the zone of Territorial Waters lie the High Seas.

Traditionally the High Seas are regarded as a sort of 'no-man's land', incapable of acquisition by any State. In this respect the High Seas are considered to be free for all nations to use them without having the right to control them. This has led to the doctrine of Freedom of the High Seas. This principle is of signal importance in peacetime, for upon it depends the free flow of oceanic trade. In time of war, however, the Freedom of the High Seas is usually the first freedom to be sacrificed by belligerent and non-belligerent alike.

The traditional limit of the extent of Territorial Waters was derived from the 'cannon-shot rule' first enunciated by Cornelius van Bynkershoek, a Dutch jurist of the 18th century. Bynkershoek argued that coastal fortresses can give effective protection against sea invaders only within range of their cannon. The principle satisfied the requirements of an age when the range of cannon-shot was no more than about a league, and so it was that the limit of Territorial Waters came to be three nautical miles from the coast.

Bynkershoek's cannon-shot rule became obsolescent with the development of improved weapons of destruction, and in the present atomic age it is all but meaningless. Since the beginning of the 20th century many maritime States have succeeded in laying claim to extend their Territorial Waters beyond the traditional three-mile limit. It is interesting to examine the reasons put forward by these States in wishing to extend their Territorial Waters at the expense of a dimimution of the extent of the High Seas.

Apart from the strategic interest dictating a State's need to define explicitly the extent of its sovereignty seawards other factors include the concern for the enforcement of customs and sanitary arrangements, the desire to control fisheries within Territorial Waters, and the aim to control the potential mineral wealth lying beneath the Territorial Waters.

A well-known and interesting example of the desire to extend Territorial Waters for strategic purposes is afforded by the Declaration of Panama issued jointly by the North and South American States in October, 1939, in the hope of preserving American neutrality during the war which had commenced a month earlier. The security zone established extended for 300 nautical miles from the American coast. The declaration, infringing as it did the principle of the Freedom of the High Seas, became null and void when the World War ended.

In 1945 the United States laid claim to sovereignty over the sea-bed of the continental shelf adjacent to her coasts. In exercising this authority oil-wells have been drilled and other mineral-working activities have appeared, in the Gulf of Mexico and other sea areas, well outside the limit of United States Territorial Waters.

Potential disputes related to claims to the sea fall into two categories. These are related respectively to Territorial Waters and continental shelves.

The width of the continental shelf varies considerably in different parts of the world. Off the north-west coast of Europe the width of the continental shelf is so great that the whole of the North Sea stands upon it. The problem of dividing the continental shelf of north-west Europe between the several States of this region who wish to stake claims to the potential mineral wealth of the North Sea bed, was not without difficulty. The discovery of rich sources of natural gas and petroleum in the bed of the North Sea made it necessary for the continental shelf of this region to be divided to the collective satisfaction of the several littoral States of North-west Europe. That this has been done successfully is a credit to the contesting States who exercised restraints in their claims, and to the wisdom and understanding of the international lawyers who were responsible for the manner in which the shelf region has been shared.

The seas and the continental shelves of the globe are the repositories of vast resources of food and mineral wealth. If this great treasure-house of natural wealth is to be tapped for the benefit of mankind as a whole, there must exist a genuine desire on the part of the world's community of nations, particularly the industrially-advanced nations, to seek just and reasonable solutions to the problems pertaining to the sovereignty of the seas.